CHESS OPENINGS 1

Queen's Raid

2 Knights Defense

Stonewall Attack

Scholastic Chess Series

Second Edition

Stephen A. Schneider

Championship Chess

Championship Chess
a division of
Teachable Tech, Inc.
3565 Evans Road
Atlanta, GA 30340
1-(888) 328-7373 (voice)
770-493-1115 (fax)
www.championshipchess.net
www.teachabletech.com

Copyright © 2002, 2005 Teachable Tech, Inc.
All rights reserved.
ISBN 0-9729456-4-4

This work is protected under current U.S. copyright laws, and the performance, display and other applicable uses of it are governed by those laws. Any uses not in conformity with the U.S. copyright statute are prohibited without our express permission, including but not limited to duplication, adaptation and transmission by television or other devices and processes. For permission, write Championship Chess, a Division of Teachable Tech, Inc. 3565 Evans Road, Atlanta, GA 30340.

Second edition, revised and enlarged 2005.

Welcome to Chess Openings 1

You are beginning a great adventure into the world of chess. Thousands of players live here. Maybe you don't know the language of this new world yet. Here, you will learn how to read, write and understand "chess."

Chess is fun and competitive. There are many opportunities to play — at home with family, at school with friends, in clubs, on the Internet and at local, state and national tournaments.

Let's get started.

You're playing White and the board is set. Your opponent is ready. What do you do first?

You're playing Black and the board is set. Your opponent makes the first move. What do you do next?

Every game starts with the opening. In *Chess Openings 1*, you'll find the things you need to know to take the advantage as the game begins — from basic concepts to detailed moves.

Playing White, you'll start an open and aggressive game. Playing Black, you'll respond to your opponent's opening moves and move to the attack.

This is the first book in our series of *Openings*, so we'll begin with the basics: **The Queen's Raid, Two Knights Defense** and **Stonewall Attack**. These aggressive, open games will put you on the offensive and make your games fun and action-filled.

In *Chess Openings 1*, you'll learn basic tactics — *pinning, forking* and *doubling up on the attack*. Step-by-step diagrams and notation will help you study and remember the openings. Activities and Puzzles give you plenty of practice in applying the openings and their variations in your games.

The companion video/DVD walks you through each opening and some of its variations with short, easy-to-follow segments. I'll coach you personally through the more complicated points and analyze the exciting moves, traps and tactics. Set your boards up and take advantage of the video coaching. Stop the action when you need to work out moves, rewind and watch again. Come back after you've tried the opening in a game and look for some finer points.

These are basic openings. There are many other, more advanced openings to discover. But first, it's most important to build a foundation and learn the fundamental patterns and principles.

It's your move,

Coach Steve Schneider

Note: We have added The Basics, pages 139-144, in case you have any trouble remembering the moves, captures, special moves or basic rules of chess!

ACKNOWLEDGMENTS

In 1974, in my home state of Georgia, there were only three scholastic tournaments. Now, there are often more than three a week. Nationwide, fewer than 100 players attended the National Elementary Championship in 1978. Now, that number has grown to over 1500 players, thanks to the efforts of many people.

I would like to acknowledge some key contributors to the success of scholastic chess with whom I have had the pleasure to work. These contributors include George Boutwell, Sylvia Chandler, Mike Decker, Rich Harris, Zvetozar Jovanovic, Boris Kogan, Richard Long, Thad Rodgers, Guillermo Ruiz, W.A. Scott, III, Colonel "Smitty" Smith, Don Schultz, David Spinks and Ted Wieber.

I would also like to thank the many parent volunteers who have made our clubs, and therefore our teaching, more helpful to scholastic players. Thanks, too, to my students and teams, especially those who became state champions and were nationally ranked by the U.S. Chess Federation. They have proven the worth of the ideas and concepts in my books.

As you go through this book, you can't help noticing our wonderful and whimsical chess characters. We are grateful to Kharam Suruma for his talents and his work in bringing chess to life.

A special thanks goes to individuals who were more directly involved in the production of these tools for scholastic players — for your time, comments and contributions: Carlos Perdomo, International Master; Terry DePeaza, former U.S. Army Champion, Life Master and 2002 Georgia Open Champion; Tim Brookshear, Expert and former Southern High School and Georgia's State Champion; Gary Southerland, Expert and National Tournament Director; Mumtaz Yusuf, active tournament player and volunteer for youth chess; and, Lew Martin, Coach of the 2002 National Elementary Championship Team.

And, most importantly, to my family and partners, Pat Schneider, Jan and Dennis Jones and Lynn Suruma: Thanks for the support, understanding, great ideas and hard work that brought this project to fruition. And, a special thanks to my son Jay, Expert and former Georgia Elementary and High School Champion, without whom I may never have gotten interested in developing chess skills for young players.

Thank you,

Coach Steve Schneider

Table of Contents

Chapter 1:	Opening Theory	1
	Activities	5
Chapter 2:	Chess Notation, An Introduction	9
	Activities	15
Chapter 3:	Chess Notation, Capturing & Special Moves	21
	Activities	27
Chapter 4:	The Queen's Raid	33
	Activities	43
Chapter 5:	En Passant	59
Chapter 6a:	The Two Knights Defense, Part 1	61
	Activities	65
Chapter 6b:	The Two Knights Defense, Part 2	69
	Activities	73
Chapter 7:	The Fork Trick	83
	Activities	87
Chapter 8:	Fried Liver Attack	95
	Activities	99
Chapter 9:	Power of the Pin	107
	Activities	109
Chapter 10:	The Stonewall	113
	Activities	119
Chapter 11:	Taking Advantage in the Opening	133
	Activities	135
The Basics		139
Glossary		145
Resources		149
Certificate		151
Parents' Guide		153

Chapter 1
Opening Theory

Let's get started.

Every game begins with an opening, but there are many openings. All openings will result in either an *open* or a *closed* game.

Closed Game

In a *closed game*, the center Pawns are blocked and do not trade. A *closed game* prevents the easy movement of pieces across the board.

Open Game

In an *open game,* center Pawns trade early. Files, or "lines of attack," are opened to allow more rapid movement of pieces across the board.

It is important for beginners to play aggressively. We recommend that scholastic players study and play *open games*. These games are more aggressive and *double-edged* — both sides have opportunities to attack and gain an advantage. They are also more fun.

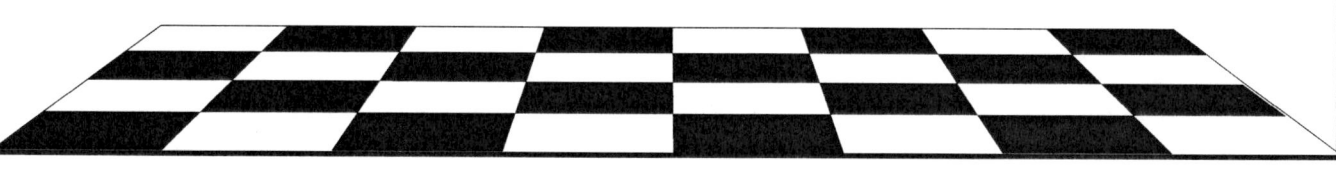

Copyright © 2002, 2005 Teachable Tech, Inc.
All Rights Reserved.

Main Principles in Chess Openings

There are 3 main principles in chess openings. They are:
1. Develop pieces, not Pawns. The Bishops, Knights and Queen come off the back rank.
2. Take control of the center. Use the pieces to attack the center.
3. Castle early and connect the Rooks. This develops the King and Rooks.

White has the advantage of the first move. To maintain that advantage, White must follow the principles of the opening.

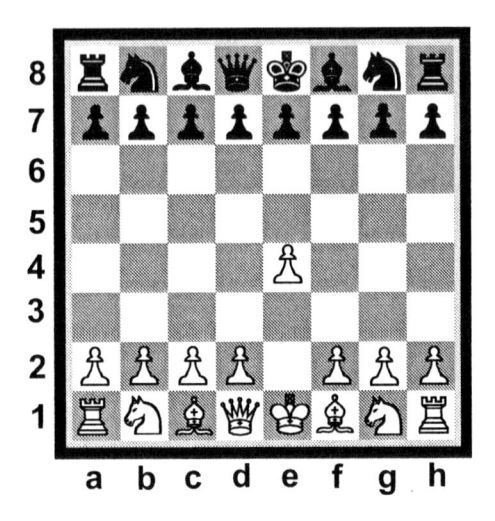

For the beginning scholastic player, the most powerful opening move for White is to move the Pawn from e2 to e4. This move attacks the center and opens the diagonals for rapid development of the Queen and Bishop. It also prevents Black's d-Pawn from safely going to d5.

This move gives White's pieces the "power of 10." On its next move, the Queen has 4 possible moves, the Bishop has 5 moves, and the Knight has 1 additional move. (The King has a move as well, but we don't want to move the King until we castle.)

Note: A move to e3 also has the *power of 10*, but it does not take control of the center.

Look at this open position:

Each side has made 3 moves. Both sides are being very aggressive, trying to take control of the center. Both sides have developed 2 pieces. White is ready to castle on the fourth move.

Note: Once you understand the principles of opening theory, you'll be able to apply it in your own games. In this book, we'll learn more about specific openings that scholastic players are most likely to see. Learn the openings and you will have the advantage!

Here are some more key points for openings.

1. Move each piece once.
2. Move only 2 or 3 Pawns.
3. Try not to move the f, g or h Pawns. They will protect the castled King.
4. Rooks stay on the back rank, either on open files or behind Pawns that are to be pushed.
5. If you can move the King and Queen Pawns safely to the center in the opening moves, do it.
6. Remember, there are exceptions to every move.

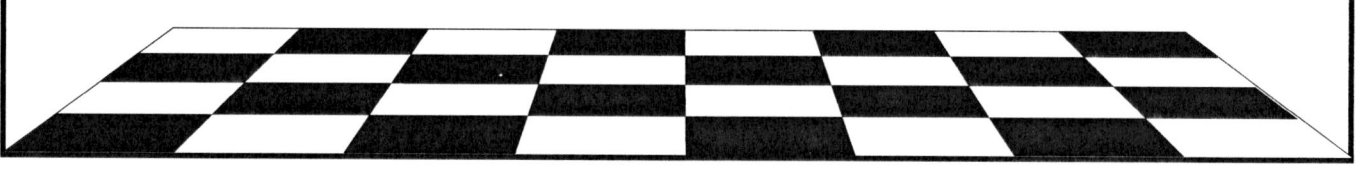

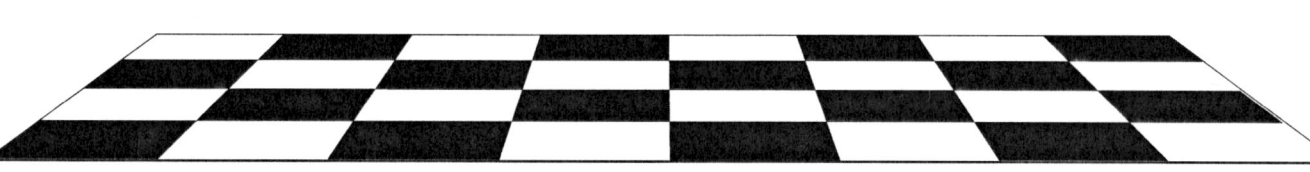

Activity 1
Opening Theory

After several moves, you can identify open and closed games from board positions.

Look at the boards below. Which one depicts an *open game*? Which one depicts a *closed game*? Why?

Position 1

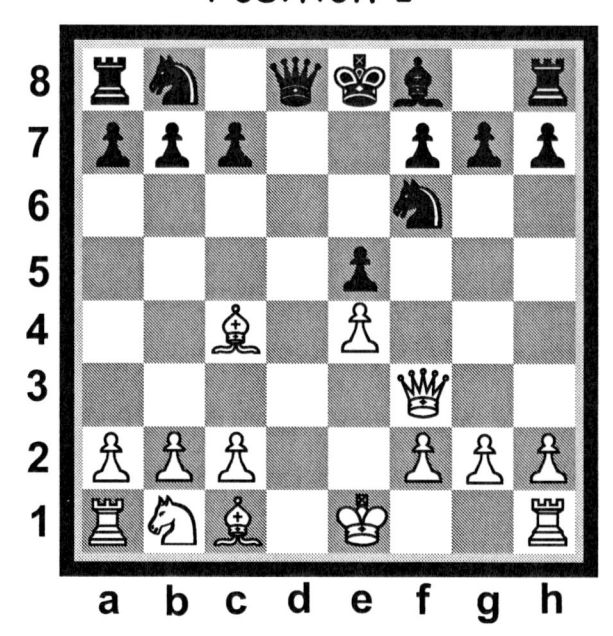

Position 2

Circle one.

Open   Closed

Circle one.

Open   Closed

Answers to Activity 1
Opening Theory

Position 1 shows an *open game.* There is an open center that comes from Pawns trading. White has developed 2 pieces, has an open diagonal for the Bishop at c1 and is ready to castle. Both sides are fighting for control of the center.

Position 2 shows a *closed game.* There are no open or half-open files. No Pawns have traded, Pawns are blocked in the center and there is very little development. Neither side is ready to castle.

Activity 2
Puzzles 1 & 2

Puzzle 1
It is White's move.

1. What move will lead to an *open game*? _____

2. What move will set up a *closed game*? _____

Puzzle 2
In Lègall's **Mate**, White checkmates in just 7 moves. White has followed the 3 main principles of openings. Black has not.

Based on this diagram:
1. How many pieces have been developed by

    White?_____ By Black?_____

2. Who is attacking or has greater control of the center?
   _____

3. Who is ready to castle? _____

4. Why could White afford to lose the Queen? _____
   _____

5. It's White's move. How can White checkmate the Black King?
   _____

Answers to Activity 2, Puzzles 1 & 2

Puzzle 1

Open Game

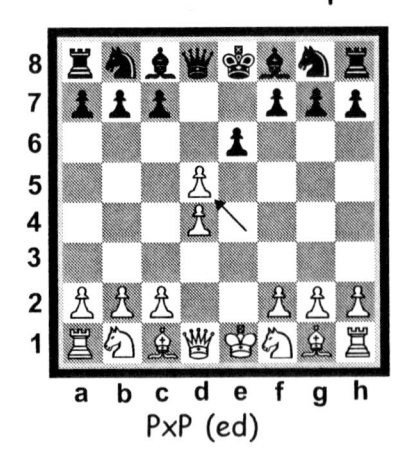

PxP (ed)

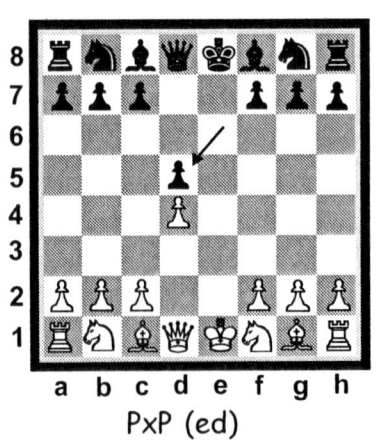

PxP (ed)

The White Pawn at e4 takes the Black Pawn at d5. Black answers by taking the White Pawn at d5 with the Black Pawn at e6.

Closed Game

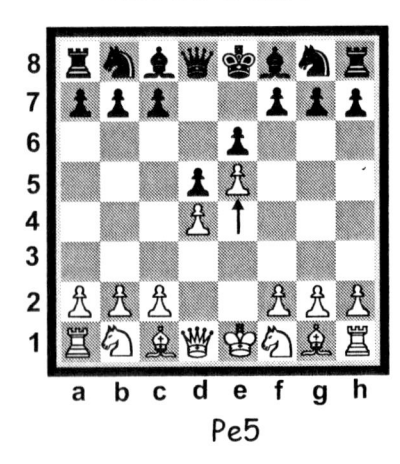

Pe5

White pushes the Pawn at e4 to e5, blocking the center file. No Pawns have been traded.

Puzzle 2 (Lègall's Mate)

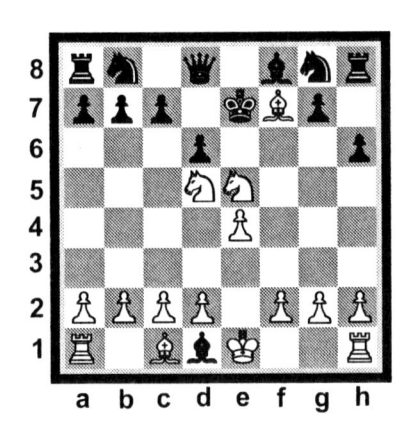

Based on this diagram:
1. White has developed 3 pieces, Black only 1.
2. White has 2 pieces in the center and is attacking the center with the Knight at c3.
3. White is ready to castle.
4. White's superior development allows checkmate, despite losing the Queen.
5. White can checkmate the Black King by moving his Knight at c3 to d5.

Note: Both White and Black have broken 1 of the rules of opening theory: Never move pieces more than once in the opening. Taking exception to this rule gives White checkmate in 7 moves.

Here is the notation for *Lègall's Mate*. If you have questions about the symbols for the moves, check the next 2 chapters on **Notation**.

	White	**Black**
1.	e4	e5
2.	Nf3	d6
3.	Bc4	h6
4.	Nc3	Bg4
5.	Nxe5	BxQ
6.	Bxf7+	Ke7
7.	Nd5#	

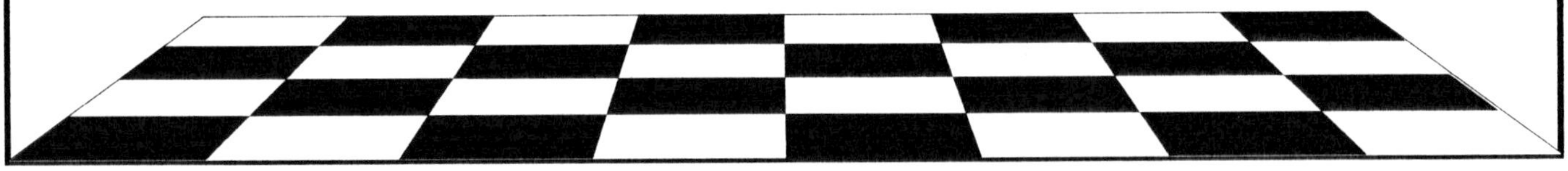

Chapter 2
Chess Notation: An Introduction

Chess players need to be able to talk about and study their games. To do this, you have to know how to read and write the language of chess — chess *notation*.

First, let's take a quick review of the algebraic grid of a chessboard.

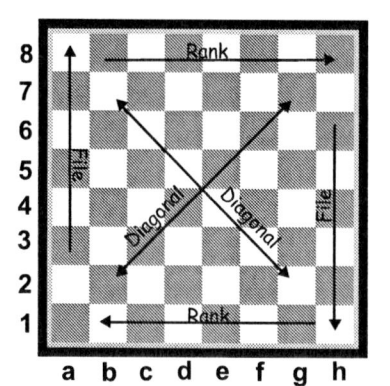

Ranks run across the board horizontally and are named by numbers, 1 through 8.

Files run up and down the board vertically and are named by lower case letters, a through h.

Diagonals can run left to right or right to left and are always made up of the same color squares.

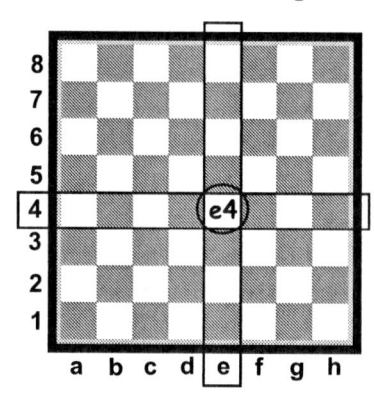

Where a file and rank intersect, a letter (file) and number (rank) designate each square on the chessboard. For example, this diagram shows the square e4.

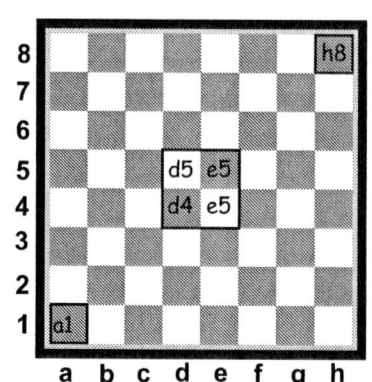

The lower left corner square is a1. The upper right square is h8. The center 4 squares are d4, e4, d5 and e5.

Always say the file letter first, then the rank number.

Remember!

Use upper case letters to designate the minor and major chess pieces:

King = K   Queen = Q   Rook = R

Bishop = B   Knight = N

Note: The King is more important so it gets the "K." and the Pawn has no letter at all. For beginners, we often use a P when showing a capture, such as PxB (Pawn catures Bishop).

At the beginning of the game, the White King (K) is at *e*1, the White Queen (Q) is at *d*1, the Queenside Bishop (B) is at *c*1, the Queenside Knight (N) is at *b*1 and the Queenside Rook (R) is at *a*1.

For Black, the King (K) is at *e*8, the Queen (Q) is at *d*8, the Kingside Bishop (B) is at *f*8, the Kingside Knight (N) is at *g*8 and the Kingside Rook (R) is at *h*8.

Note: The Queens stand on their own color — White Queen on a light square, Black Queen on a dark square.

Because there are so many Pawns, they are not designated by a capital letter, but by the file on which they stand. The Queen Pawn is on the d-file. The Kingside Rook Pawn is on the h-file, etc.

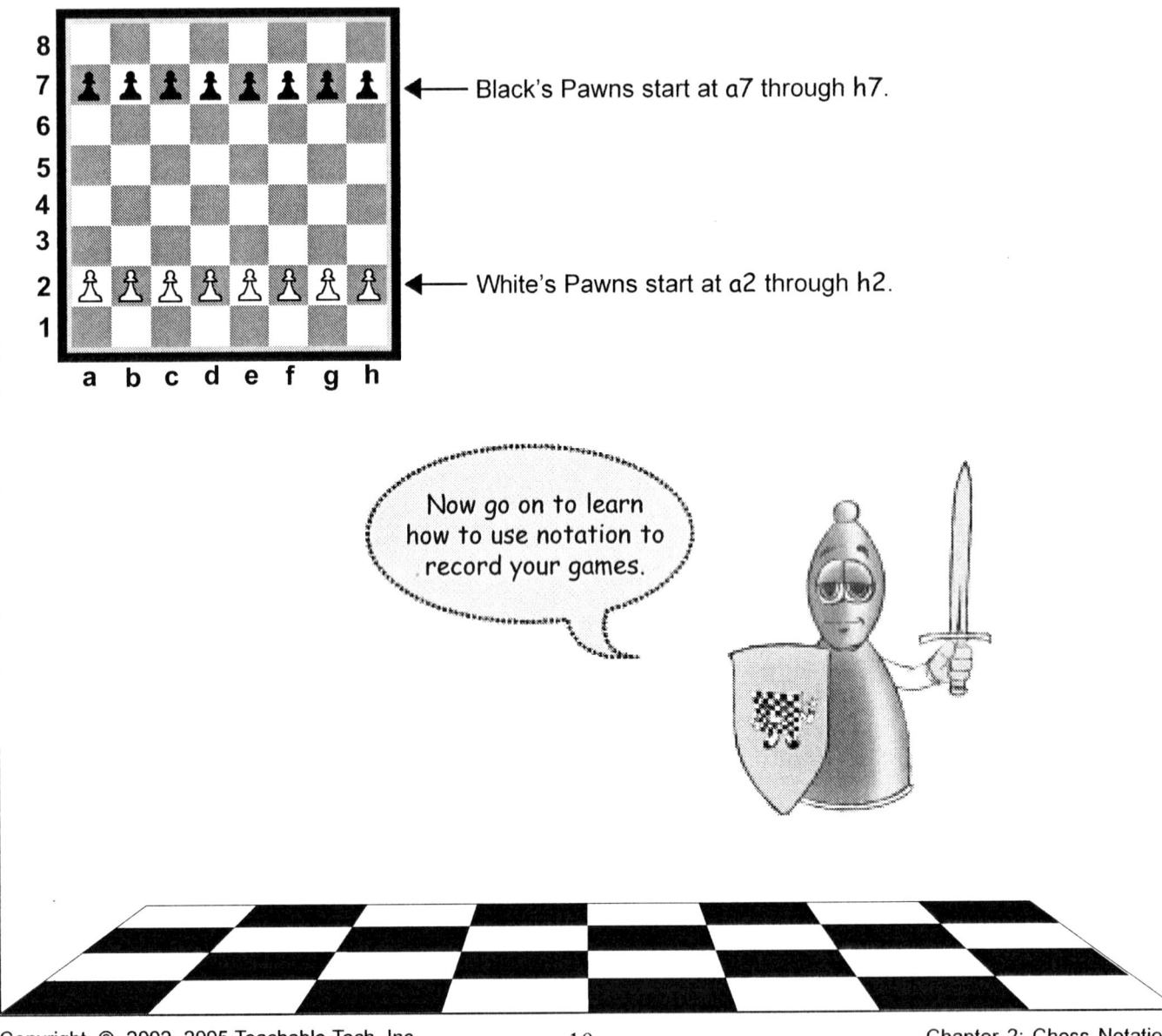

← Black's Pawns start at *a*7 through *h*7.

← White's Pawns start at *a*2 through *h*2.

Now go on to learn how to use notation to record your games.

Copyright © 2002, 2005 Teachable Tech, Inc.
All Rights Reserved.

Chapter 2: Chess Notation
An Introduction

Notation

You will use *notation* when you record your games.

Chess games are recorded in a scorebook or on a score sheet. The top part of the sheet lets you describe the event or where the game takes place. It could be in class, at camp, in your chess club or at home, as well as at an official tournament.

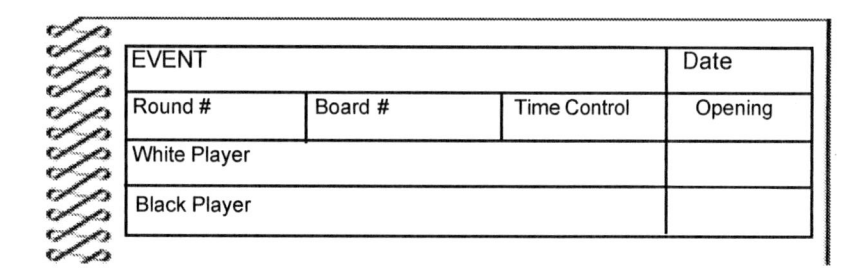

EVENT			Date
Round #	Board #	Time Control	Opening
White Player			
Black Player			

Each move of a game is numbered on the main section of a chess score sheet. Usually, the score sheet is divided into several columns. White moves first, so its moves are always listed first in the left column; Black's moves are always listed in the right column.

#	WHITE	BLACK	#	WHITE	BLACK
1			16		
2			17		
3			18		
4			19		

Moves are designated by the square to which the player moved. Let's look at the first few moves of a game and its notation on a score sheet.

On the first move, White moves the *e*-Pawn at *e*2 (2 spaces to *e*4). Black moves the *e*-Pawn at *e*7 (2 spaces to *e*5).

#	WHITE	BLACK	#	WHITE	BLACK
1	e4	e5	16		
2			17		
3			18		
4			19		

On the second move, White moves the Kingside Knight to f3; Black moves the Queenside Knight to c6. Now, the e5 Pawn is protected from attack by White's Knight.

#	WHITE	BLACK	#	WHITE	BLACK
1	e4	e5	16		
2	Nf3	Nc6	17		
3			18		
4			19		

As you can see, Pawn moves are designated only by the square to which the Pawns move. Moves by pieces are designated by the symbol for the piece and the square to which it moves.

If the White Bishop moves to c4 on the third move, it would be written as Bc4. If Black's Knight moves to f6, it would be written as Nf6.

#	WHITE	BLACK	#	WHITE	BLACK
1	e4	e5	16		
2	Nf3	Nc6	17		
3	Bc4	Nf6	18		
4			19		

Castling is a special move. Its notation describes whether castling takes place Kingside or Queenside.

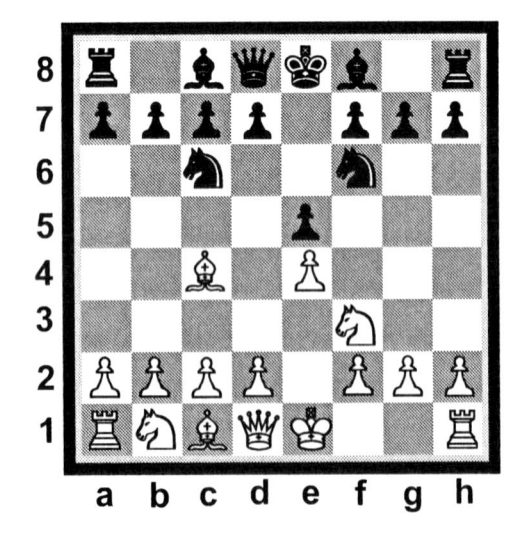

Here, White is ready to castle Kingside. There are 2 empty squares between the King and Rook. Kingside castling is written as 0-0, the 2 zeroes depicting the 2 empty squares.

4. 0-0

Remember: To castle, first the King moves 2 squares toward the Rook and then, the Rook jumps to the other side of the King.

In this position White is ready to castle Queenside. There are 3 empty squares between the King and Rook. Queenside castling is written as 0-0-0, depicting the 3 empty squares.

0-0-0

Note: For Queenside castling, the zeros mean that there are 3 empty spaces between the King and the Rook.

In the game that led to White castling Queenside, players had made the following moves.

#	WHITE	BLACK	#	WHITE	BLACK
1	d4	d5	16		
2	Bf4	Bf5	17		
3	Nc3	Nc6	18		
4	Qd2	Nf6	19		
5	0-0-0				

Activity 3
Chess Notation, An Introduction

It's important to be able to name each square and the position of each piece during a chess game.

Write the notation for each designated position and its piece.

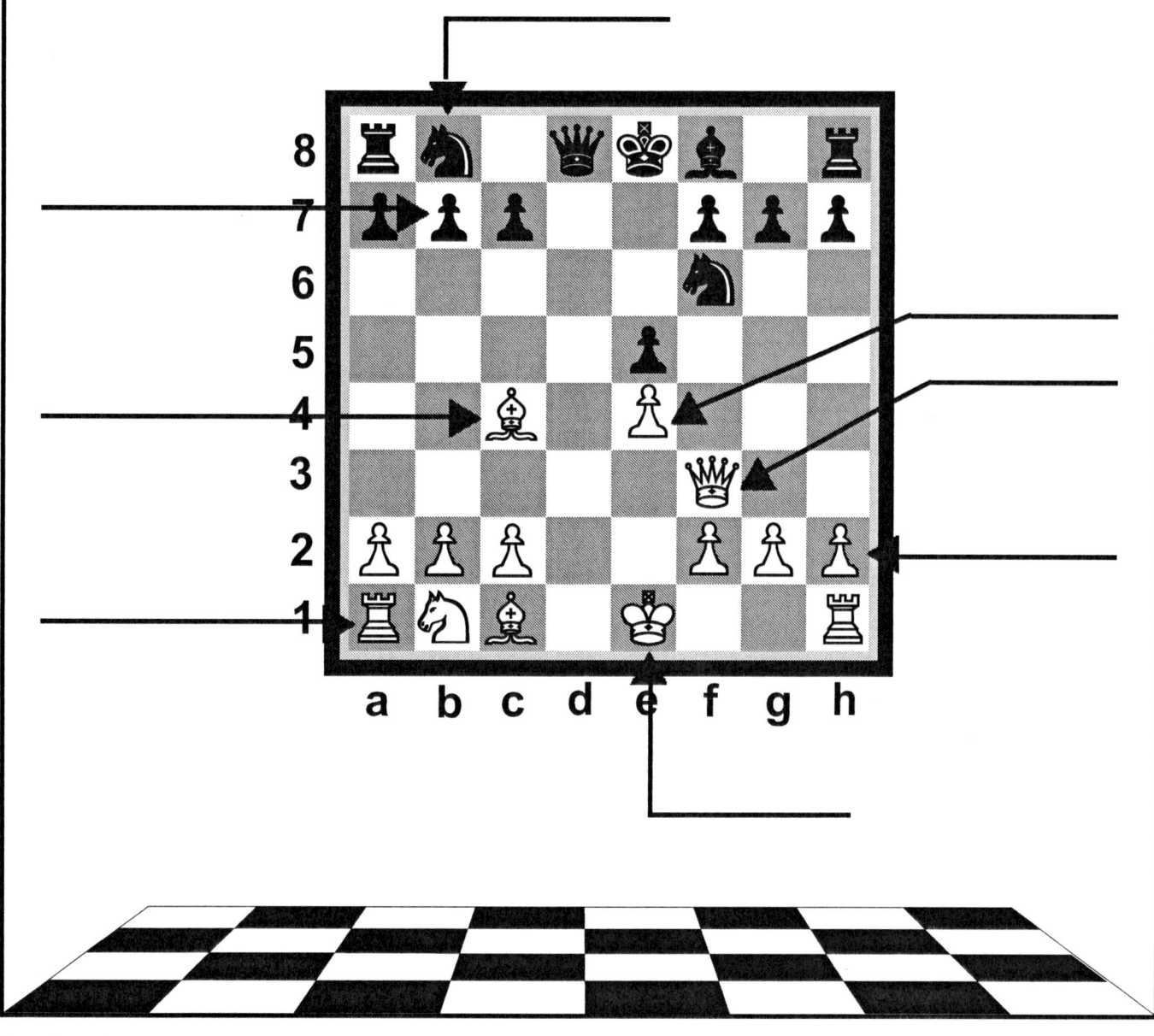

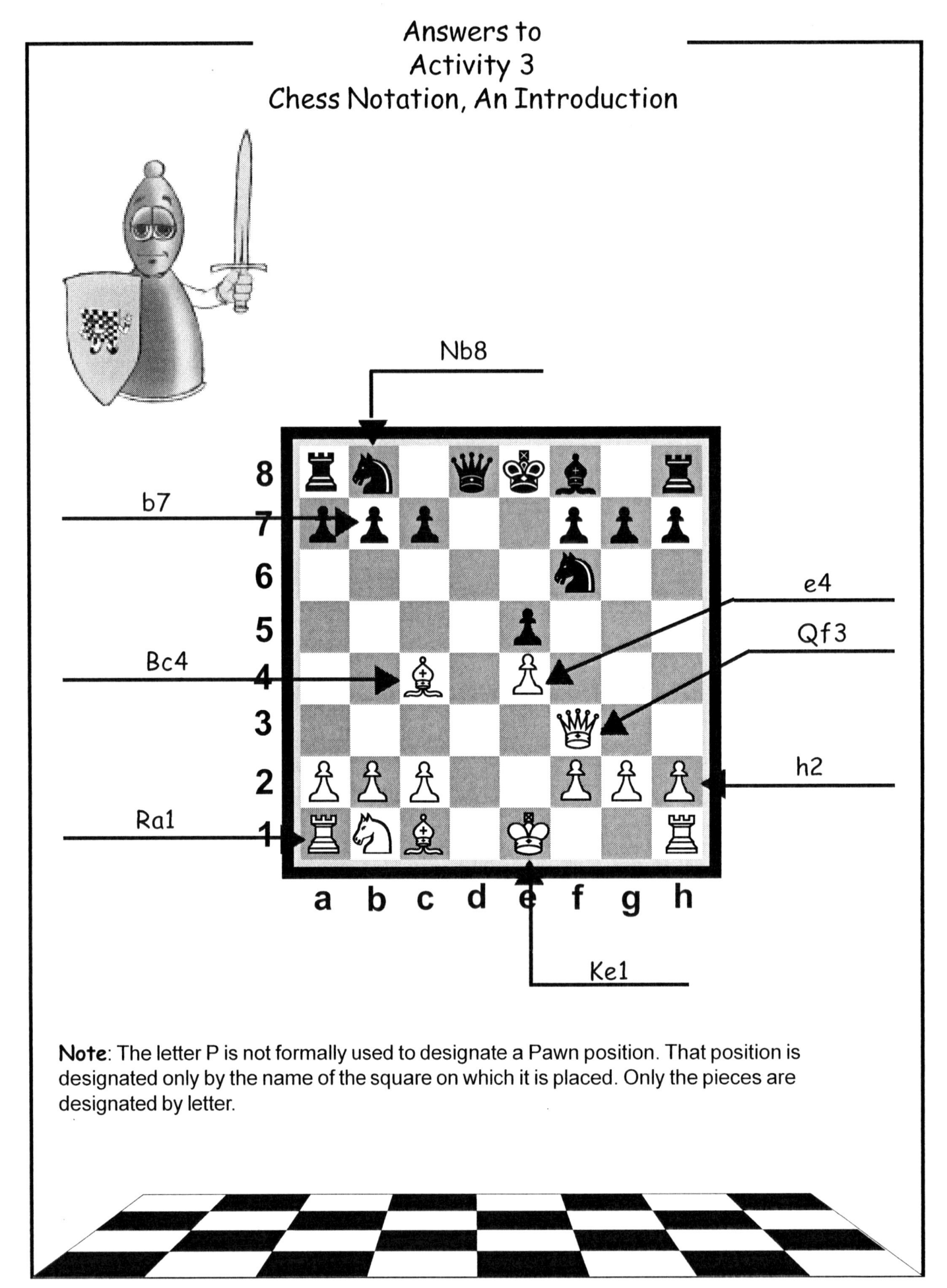

Answers to Activity 3
Chess Notation, An Introduction

Nb8

b7

Bc4

e4

Qf3

h2

Ra1

Ke1

Note: The letter P is not formally used to designate a Pawn position. That position is designated only by the name of the square on which it is placed. Only the pieces are designated by letter.

Activity 4
Chess Notation, An Introduction

Use the score sheet to write the notation for the first 4 moves of the game below.

#	WHITE	BLACK	#	WHITE	BLACK
1	e4	e5	16		
2			17		
3			18		
4			19		

Move 1

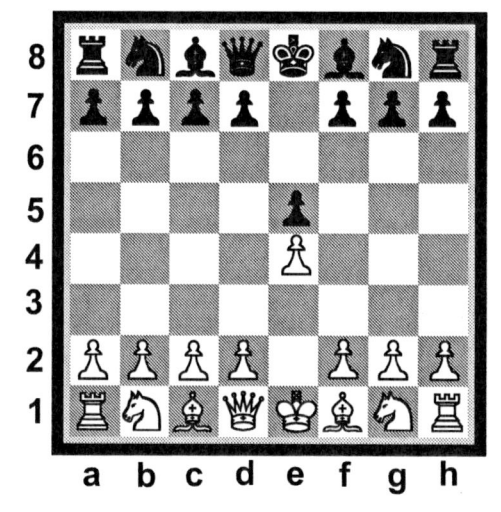

Move 2

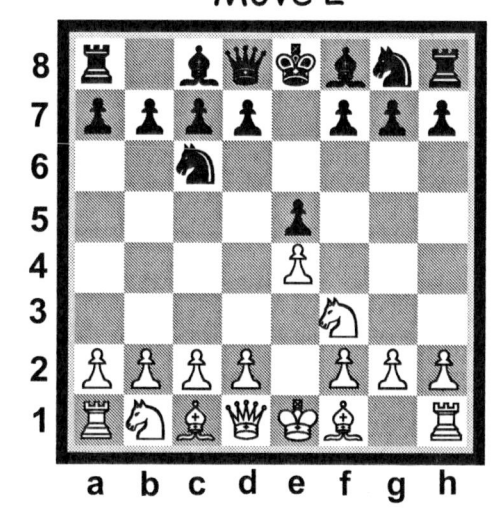

Move 3

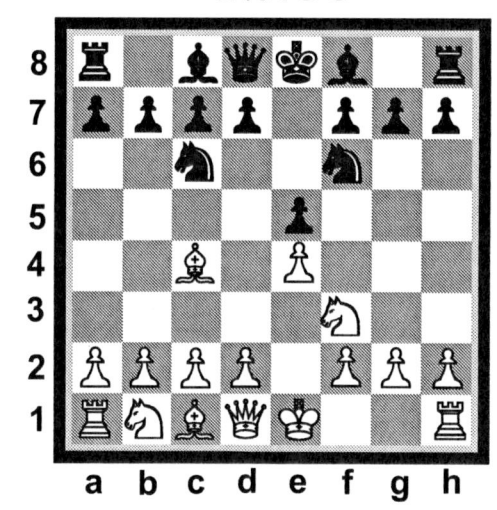

Move 4

Answers to Activity 4
Chess Notation, An Introduction

EVENT					Date	
Round #		Board #		Time Control	Opening	
White Player						
Black Player						

#	WHITE	BLACK	#	WHITE	BLACK
1	e4	e5	15		
2	Nf3	Nc6	16		
3	Bc4	Nf6	17		
4	0-0	Bc5	18		
5			19		
6			20		
7			21		
8			22		
9			23		
10			24		
11			25		
12			26		
13			27		
14			28		

Notation Sheet

EVENT				Date	
Round #		Board #	Time Control	Opening	
White Player					
Black Player					

#	WHITE	BLACK	#	WHITE	BLACK
1			15		
2			16		
3			17		
4			18		
5			19		
6			20		
7			21		
8			22		
9			23		
10			24		
11			25		
12			26		
13			27		
14			28		

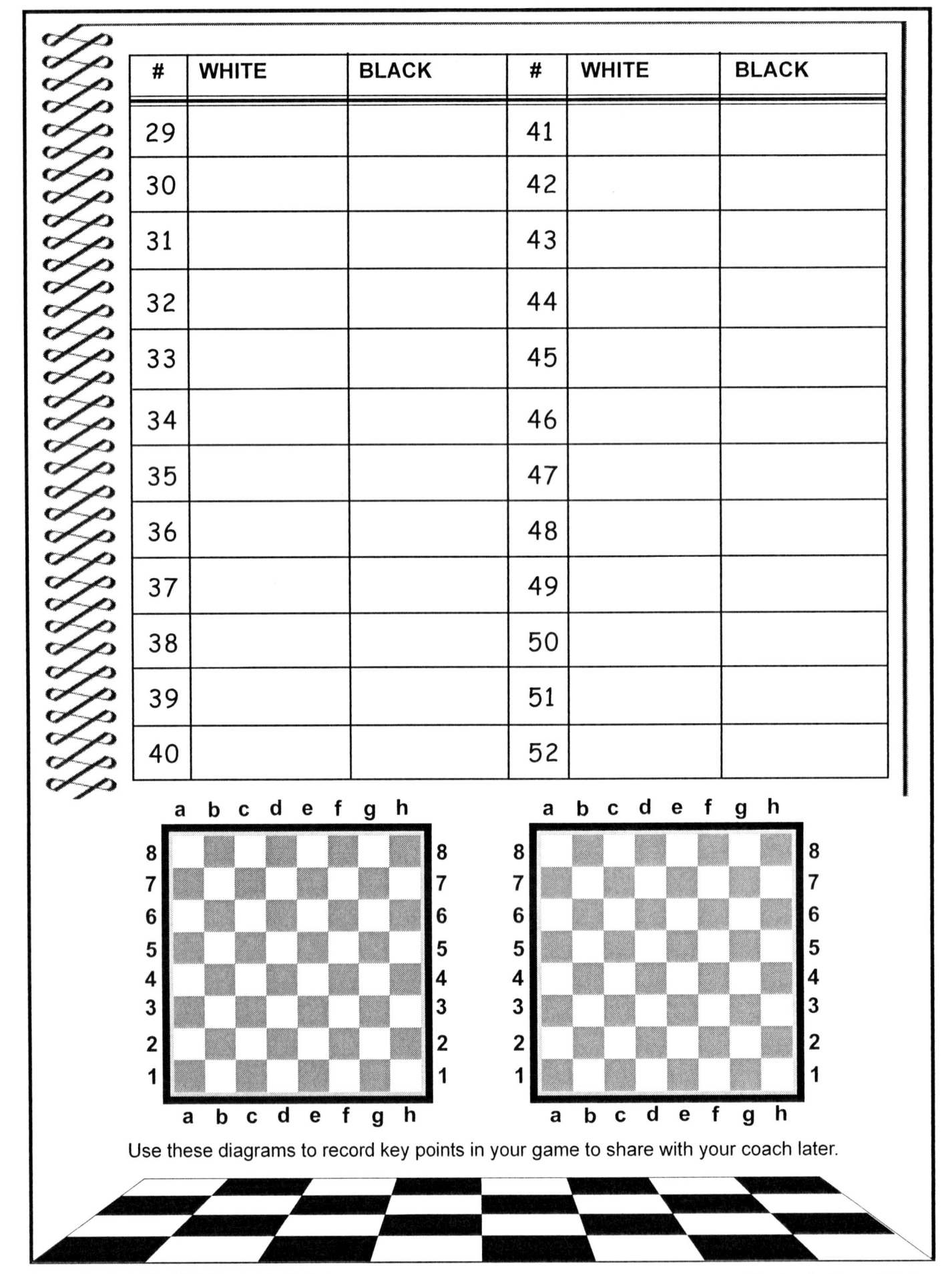

#	WHITE	BLACK	#	WHITE	BLACK
29			41		
30			42		
31			43		
32			44		
33			45		
34			46		
35			47		
36			48		
37			49		
38			50		
39			51		
40			52		

Use these diagrams to record key points in your game to share with your coach later.

Chapter 3
Chess Notation, Capturing & Special Moves

There are a few more symbols you must know.

The first symbol is the "x" for capturing.

A capture can be indicated with an "x." **BxN** means Bishop takes Knight; **QxR** means Queen takes Rook. However, there are several times in a game when notation must be clarified.

If a piece is actually attacking 2 or more of the same pieces, you should specify the location of the piece to make it clear which one was captured. For example:

Example 1

White's Bishop can take the Knight at c6 or the Knight at e4: **BxNc6** or **BxNe4**. The notation **BxN** wouldn't tell you which Knight the Bishop took.

Example 2

White's Queen is attacking 3 different Black pawns: one at h7, one at f7 and one at e5. An attack by the White Queen on the:

☆ Black Pawn at h7 would be recorded: **Qxh7**

☆ Black Pawn at f7 would be recorded: **Qxf7+**

☆ Black Pawn at e5 would be recorded: **Qxe5+**

Example 3

There are several ways to indicate a Pawn capture.

Before the Capture

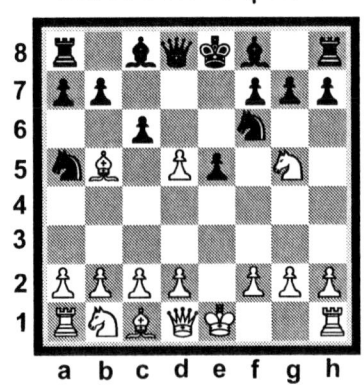

After the Capture

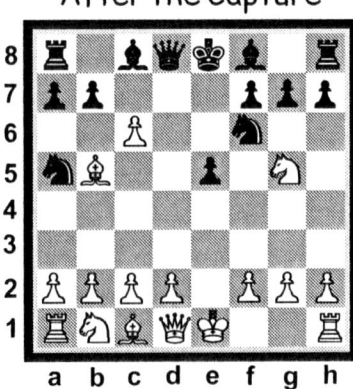

If the Pawn at d5 captures the Pawn at c6, it can be written as: **dc or dxc or PxP**.

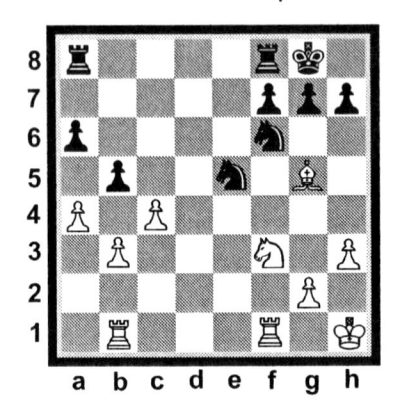

Note: The most "officially correct" notation is **dc**. Many scholastic players use the "x" to indicate a capture — **dxc**. Young beginners may want to use **PxP** (Pawn takes Pawn) as they begin notation. But, be careful. Often, there is more than one possible move or capture by a Pawn or a piece. There are 2 specific cases where you must be careful how you record your move.

Case 1: Both Knights or Rooks can move to the same square.

Black Rook moves: moving a Rook to b8 to protect the Pawn at b5. Either Rook can go to b8, therefore Rb8 is not sufficient. Correct notation is Rab8 or Rfb8.

Black Knight moves: moving one of the Knights to protect the other. For example, both Knights can move to d7, therefore Nd7 is not sufficient. Here you would write either N4d7 or N3d7 or Ned7 or Nfd7.

Case 2: One Pawn can capture 1 of 2 Pawns.

Black Pawn move: The Pawn at b5 can capture either the Pawn at a4 or at c4. PxP is not sufficient notation. You'll have to record the capture by the name of the squares. For example: **ba** or **bc** is the notation of choice. But, for beginners who like to see captures (x's) on their score sheets, you may use PxPa or Pxa; or, in the second case, PxPc or Pxc.

Remember!
Your notation must record the move clearly so that you can replay and study your games.

The road to chess success is paved with notation pads!

Notation: En Passant

En Passant is a special move. It is important to understand how it works and how to write it.

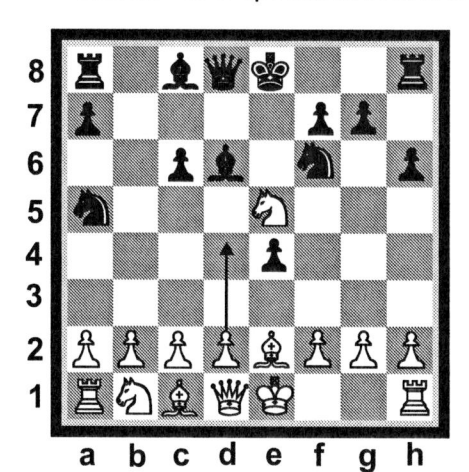

It's White's move.

d4

White moved the Pawn at d2 two spaces to d4.

The White Pawn passed through d3, a square "attacked" by Black's Pawn at e4.

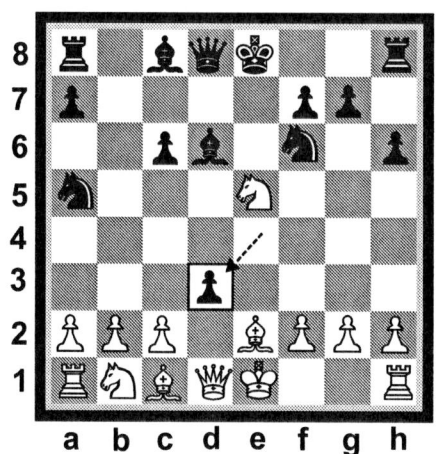

...   **ed e.p. or (exd e.p. or PxP e.p.)**

On the next move only, Black may claim to have captured White's Pawn "in passing" — *en passant* — as it crosses the d3 square. It is written as **e.p.**

En passant can happen:
1. only between 2 Pawns;
2. only if a Pawn moves 2 spaces;
3. only if an opponent's Pawn is on the adjacent file and on the same rank after an opponent's move; and,
4. only if the capture takes place immediately following the Pawn's move.

Note: *En passant* is a relatively new rule in chess. When chess first began, Pawns could only move one square at a time. To speed up the game, the rule changed during the Renaissance to allow Pawns to move 2 squares on the first move. Since this move often "passed by" a potential attacker, the *en passant* rule was established.

✯ For activities with *en passant* see **Chapter 5**.

Notation: More Special Moves

Pawn Promotion

"Pawn Promotion," often called "Queening a Pawn," is another special move. If a Pawn gets to the opposite side of the board, it **must** be promoted to any piece, except King. If a Pawn chooses to become a Queen, the move is annotated by the square the Pawn moved to and, in parentheses, the piece it changed into.
For example: **b8 (Q)** or **g1 (R)**

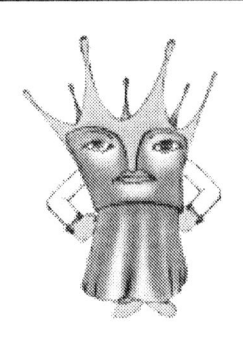

Note: A player could have as many as 9 Queens in a game.

Check and Checkmate

To show that a move has placed the opponent's King in check, add a "+" to the end of the notation. For example:

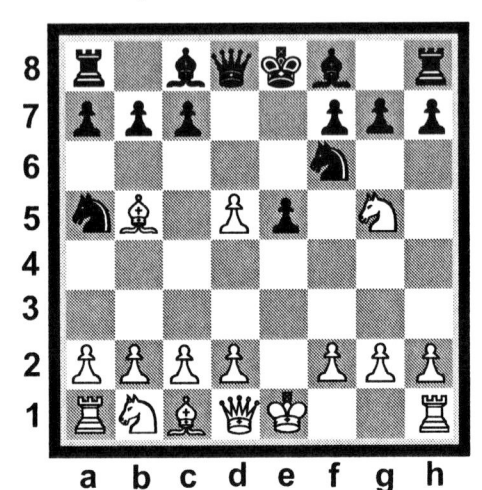

Bb5+

The White Bishop moved to b5, attacking the King, and put Black's King in check.

To show that a move has placed the opponent's King in checkmate, add "++" or "#" to the end of the notation. For example:

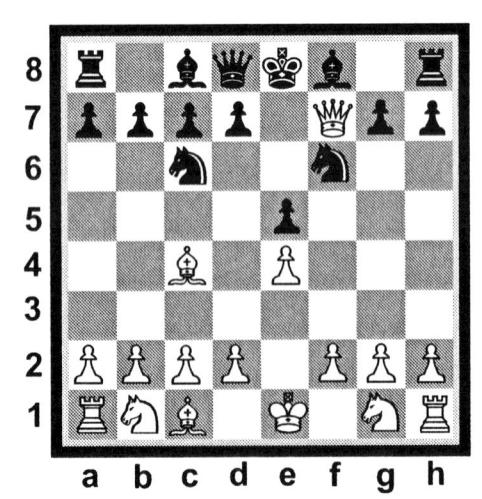

Qxf7# (preferred) or **Qxf7++**

The White Queen moved to f7 and put the Black King in checkmate.

Remember!
This is how the game ends. The King is trapped, **not** taken off the board.

Chapter 3: Chess Notation, Capturing & Special Moves

Notation: Bad or Terrible Move

When a player makes a bad move, place a "?" at the end of the notation. Add more question marks for a really bad move, as when a move leads to checkmate.

3. ...   Nf6???

On the third move, Black moved the Knight to f6, attacking White's Queen at h5 and the Pawn at d4.

Black did not notice that both White's Bishop at c4 and the Queen at h5 are attacking the Pawn at f7, protected only by the King. If the White Queen takes the Pawn (Qxf7#), Black's King is in checkmate.

Black should have moved the Pawn at g7 to g6, attacking the Queen and forcing a retreat. There are other moves that would stop the checkmate.

Note: Often, when reading chess books, you'll notice "..." next to the number of the move. This means that White's move had already been described, so you are looking at only Black's move.

Other Notation Punctuation

Note: The following notation punctuation is optional. This punctuation is used more to describe the soundness of a move, rather than specify thenew position on the board.

!   The only right move; a very good move
!? A surprising move; may or may not be a good move
?! A dubious move

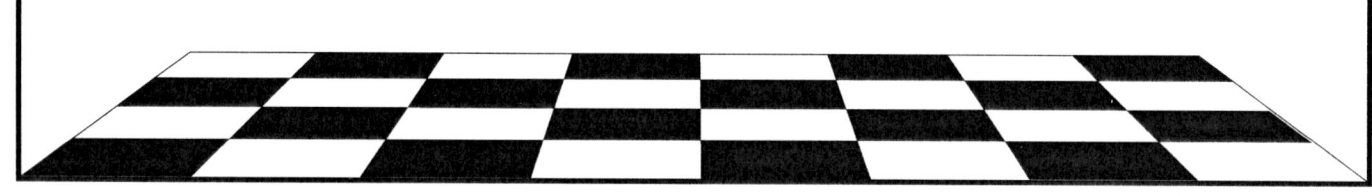

Activity 5
Chess Notation, Capturing & Special Moves

Can you track the action of a chess game? Read the notation for the opening below. Then, show the position of the board after 12 moves.

#	White	Black	#	White	Black
1	e4	e5	8	Be2	h6
2	Nf3	Nc6	9	Nf3	e4
3	Bc4	Nf6	10	Ne5	Bd6
4	Ng5	d5	11	d4	ed e.p. / exd e.p. / PxP e.p.
5	ed / exd / PxP)	Na5			
6	Bb5+	c6	12	Nxd3	0-0
7	dc / dxc / PxP	bc / bxc / PxP	13		

Now, show the position of the board after 12 moves. Use the abbreviations for each piece. Designate the chess piece colors with the letters B for Black and W for White. For example, at the end of the moves there is a Black Knight on f6 as shown below.

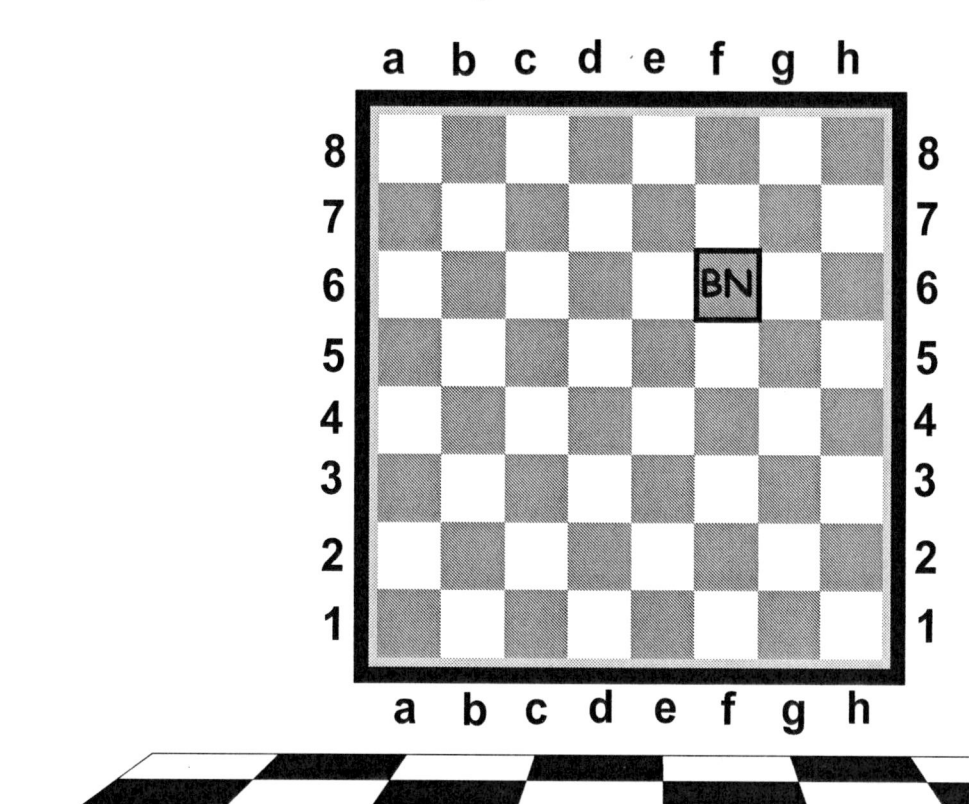

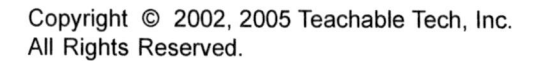

[Chess board diagram with BN on f6]

Answer to
Activity 5: Chess Notation, Capturing & Special Moves

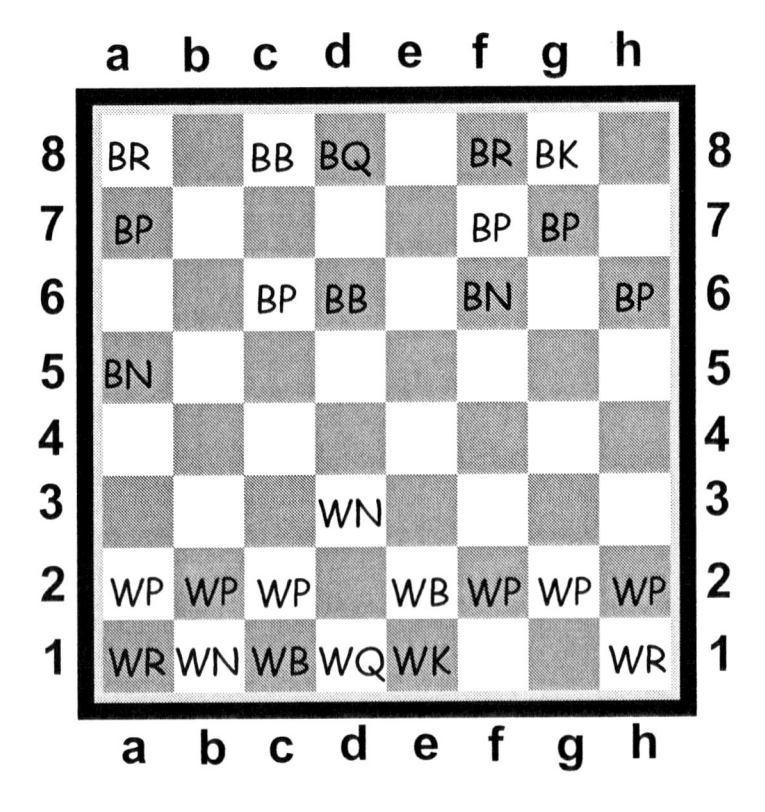

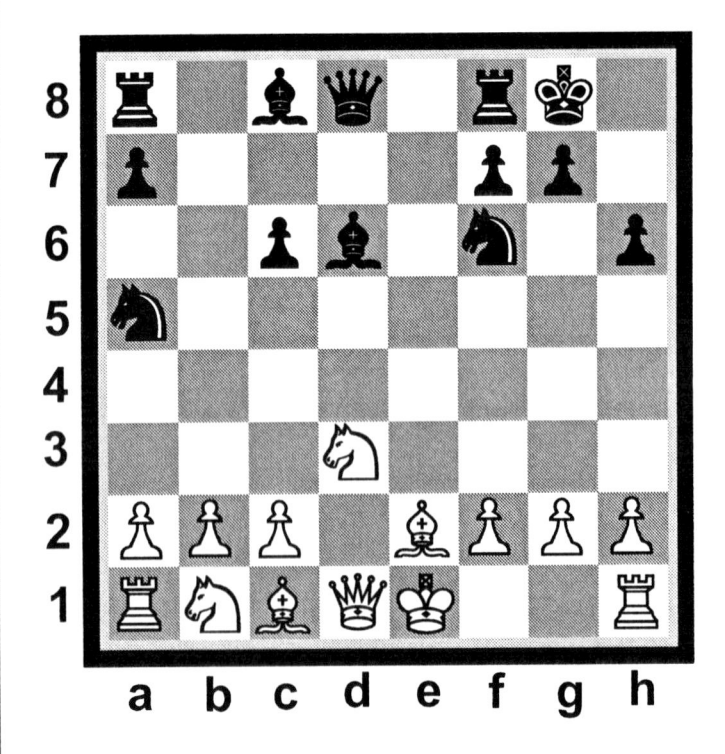

	a	b	c	d	e	f	g	h	
8	BR		BB	BQ		BR	BK		8
7	BP					BP	BP		7
6			BP	BB		BN		BP	6
5	BN								5
4									4
3				WN					3
2	WP	WP	WP		WB	WP	WP	WP	2
1	WR	WN	WB	WQ	WK			WR	1
	a	b	c	d	e	f	g	h	

This is how the chessboard will look at the end of the 12th move. Were your abbreviations correct?

Activity 6
Chess Notation, Sequencing Moves

Here is the final position of a 4-move Queen's Raid game that ends in checkmate. Fill in the score sheet below to show the notation. Put the moves in a potentially correct sequence. For example, it's impossible to move a Bishop before you move a Pawn; however, you could move either a Knight or a Pawn first.

Notice: White's Queen moves twice.

#	White	Black	#	White	Black
1			5		
2			6		
3			7		
4		xxx	8		

Answer to
Activity 6: Chess Notation, Sequencing Moves

NOTE: This is the correct order of moves for the **Queen's Raid** explained in Chapter 4.

#	White	Black	#	White	Black
1	e4	e5	5		
2	Qh5	Nc6	6		
3	Bc4	Nf6???	7		
4	Qxf7#		8		

Activity 7
Chess Notation

The diagram below shows the position of the board after 8 moves are completed. No pieces have been captured or traded. No piece has moved more than once. Fill in the score sheet to show the notation. Once again put the moves in a possibly correct sequence.

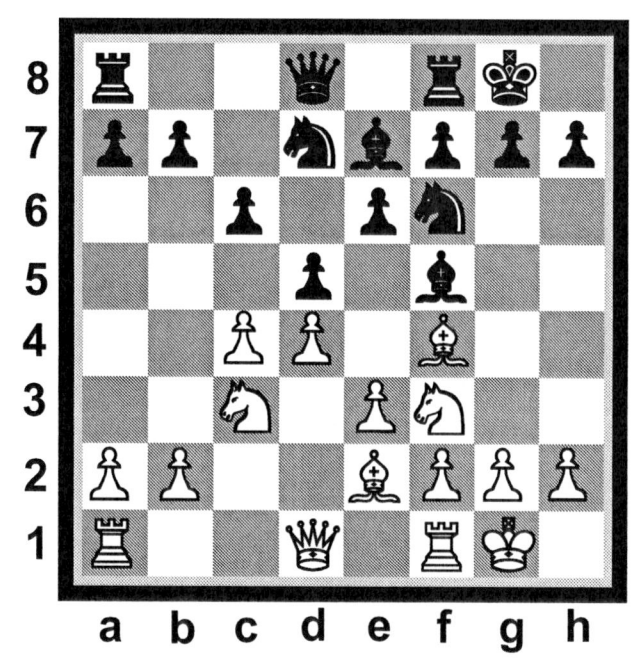

#	White	Black	#	White	Black
1			5		
2			6		
3			7		
4			8		

Answers to Activity 7 Chess Notation

#	White	Black	#	White	Black
1	d4	d5	5	e3	Be7
2	c4	c6	6	Be2	Nf6
3	Bf4	Bf5	7	Nf3	0-0
4	Nc3	e6	8	0-0	Nbd7

Chapter 4
The Queen's Raid

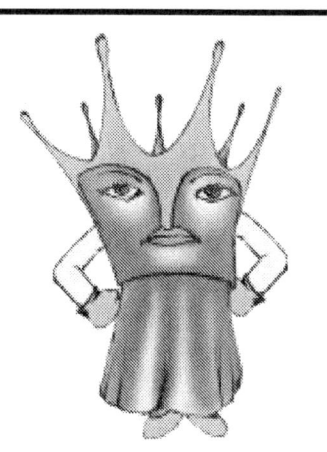

The first opening strategy most beginners see is the *Queen's Raid*. This opening can lead to a quick checkmate, in 4 moves, or the capture of a Rook, also in 4 moves. It is also the first opening that scholastic players must learn to stop. Throughout the Queen's Raid, we will focus on the **best** play for White.

The Queen's Raid lets you play a double-edged, aggressive game using many important *tactics* — combination of short-term moves, leading to a better position or material gain.

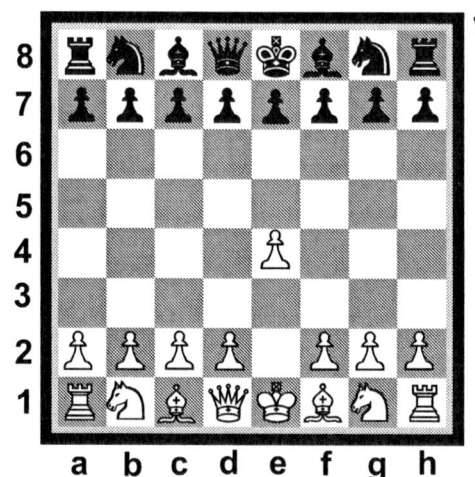

White	Black
1. e4	

For the beginning scholastic player, the most powerful opening move for White is e4.

This move gives White the "power of 10." (See Chapter 1, Opening Theory, page 2.) This move also prevents Black from safely moving his Queen Pawn out to d5.

1. ...	e5

Black's most powerful move here is e5. The Black Queen, Bishop, King and Knight all have the same moves as White on the next move. This has also blocked White's King Pawn and prevents White from safely moving to d4 to control the center.

Note: With this move, both Black and White compete for control of the center. Players have prepared for rapid development of pieces that will allow them to castle early.

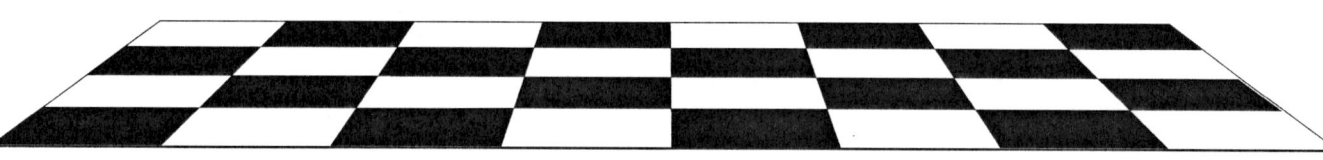

2. Qh5

The opening is called the Queen's Raid, so bring out the Queen as soon as possible. Place it where it attacks Black's undefended Pawn at e5 and Black's Pawn at f7, which is protected only by the King. Because the Queen is the most powerful piece, bringing it out early gives White the most power.

Note: Many chess openings played by the top players bring out the Queen early. Part of good opening development has the Queen move off the back rank.

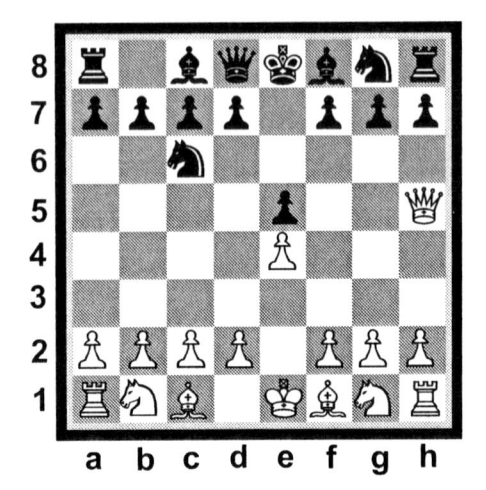

2. ...   Nc6

The beginner's best move is to both develop a piece and protect the Pawn at e5. Black's best piece to develop is the Knight to c6, rather than the Queen, Bishop or Pawn.

Note: However, a very common response for Black is to attack the Queen with the Pawn at g7. If Black moves the Pawn to g6, attacking the Queen, White takes the unprotected Pawn at e5 with check and wins the unprotected Rook on the next move.

3. Bc4

This move helps White maintain the opening advantage, keeping Black on the defensive. Now, 2 pieces attack the Pawn at f7.

Note: This is one of the first tactics that new players learn — 2 pieces attacking and taking advantage of the weakness of f7 because it is only protected by the King. The same applies for Black attacking at f2.

This is what happens if Black does not know how to stop the Queen's Raid!

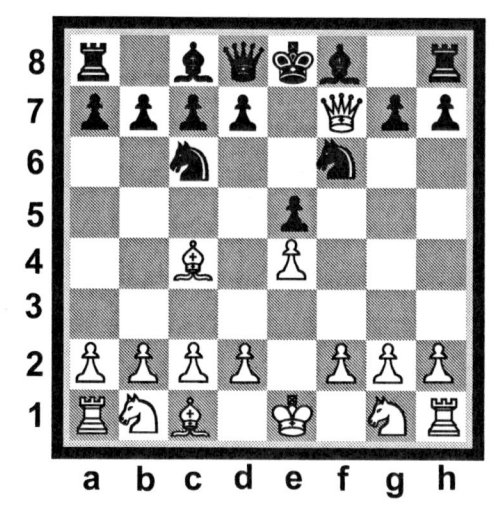

3. ...   **Nf6???**

This move looks good. Black develops a piece, attacks the center, prepares to castle and attacks the Queen at h5. But, that's exactly what White hopes will happen and Black loses the game immediately.

4. Qxf7#

Capturing the Pawn at f7 is checkmate.

This is often called **Scholar's Mate** or "Checkmate in Four." It's not the quickest checkmate possible, but it's the most popular with beginning players.

Remember the first moves of the opening.

1. e4   e5
2. Qh5   Nc6
3. Bc4

Now, let's see how Black can stop the Queen's Raid.

Stopping The Queen's Raid

3. ...   **g6**

This is the best move to stop White's attack.

Note: We try not to move the f, g and h Pawns in the opening because this is where we intend to castle. This is one of the many exceptions.

Two other moves are Qe7 and Qf6. These moves are not as good because they block good squares for the Bishop at f8 and the Knight at g8.

4. Qf3   **Nf6**

With the Queen at f3, White is still threatening checkmate at f7.

Black's best move to stop the threat is to bring the Knight to f6 to block the attack. This move also attacks the center, develops a piece and prepares to castle.

It is important to look at the board and understand why you make each move. For example, in Move 3 Nf6 was the very worst move you could make. But, in Move 4, it is the **best** move.

5. Ne2   **Bg7**

Black's plan is to move the Knight to d4. White prevents this plan by moving Knight to e2. (If Black moves Nd4 now, it's traded off (NxN and PxN)). Black's move Bg7 protects the Knight and prepares to castle. The Bishop completes the fortress that will guard the castled King.

Case 1: Better Defense for White

White's next move is to c3. The moves that follow are a more defensive **line** of the Queen's Raid. It has less risk for White.

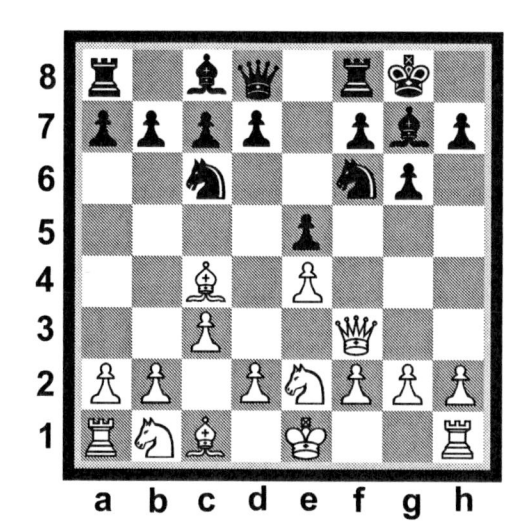

6. c3   **0-0**

White's move to c3 prevents Black's Knight from coming into b4 or d4.

Black castles.

line: a planned set of moves recognized by many players.

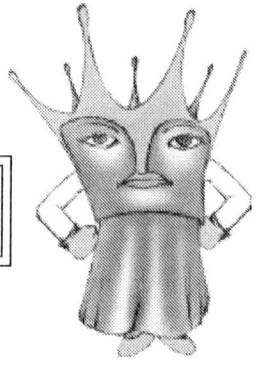

7. d3   **d6**

White's move to d3 allows White to develop the Bishop and maintain control of the center.

Black's move to d6 also opens the path for the Bishop.

Note: If Black had moved d6 before White moved d3, White would have to move h3 to keep Black's Bishop from coming to g4, attacking White's Queen.

Note: White has not yet castled. But, White can choose to castle either side, depending on how the game progresses.

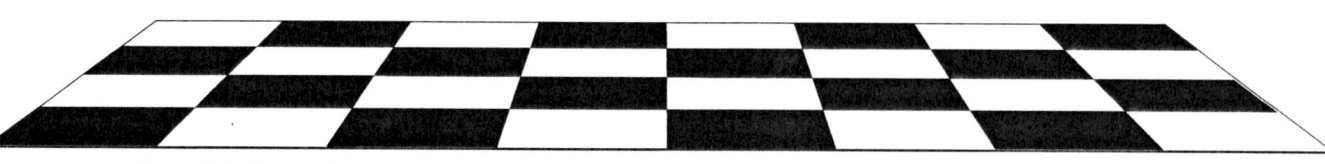

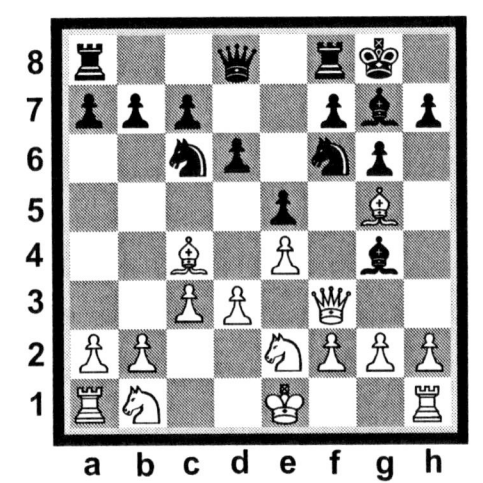

8. Bg5	Bg4?

White and Black both develop Bishops to good squares.

For White, the Black Knight is now pinned to the Queen. Black gets the last piece developed and it looks like a good move to attack the Queen. In fact, it is a possible trap White sets for Black.

The following moves show how the trap works.

9. BxN	BxQ
10. BxQ	BxN
11. Bxc7	Bg4
12. Bxd6	Rfd8

White is now up 2 Pawns, has not yet castled, but has the choice of castling either side, depending on how the game progresses.

Often, White can end up a piece ahead, depending on Black's play. Follow these steps after Move 9 above:

10. BxQ	RxB
11. PxB	

White is now a piece ahead because Black didn't make the best move once Black was in the trap.

Now, let's look at a more aggressive line for White than c3 at move 6. Let's review these moves.

#	WHITE	BLACK	#	WHITE	BLACK
1	e4	e5	16		
2	Qh5	Nc6	17		
3	Bc4	g6	18		
4	Qf3	Nf6	19		
5	Ne2	Bg7			

Case 2: A More Aggressive Line

6. d3   **d6**

For White, d3 is a more aggressive line because it sets up a more rapid development of pieces.

For Black, d6 is the usual development.

Note: If Black had moved d6 before White moved d3, White would have to move h3 to keep Black's Bishop from coming to g4, attacking White's Queen.

7. Bg5   **0-0**

For White, Bg5 develops the Bishop, creates a double attack on the Knight and *pins* the Knight to the Queen Usually, *pinning* the Knight to the Queen **before** an opponent has castled is not a good move. But, in this case, the double attack makes it a better move.

Castling is always a good developing move.

8. Nbc3   **Bg4**

White develops a piece and threatens to go to d5 for a triple attack on the pinned Knight.

Black's move develops the Bishop and attacks White's Queen. It looks good, but is actually the same possible trap as in *Case 1* (Move 6. c3), page 37.

Pin: an attack against 2 or more of an opponent's pieces in a straight line — diagonal, rank or file — where the piece behind is of greater value so, if the front piece (the *pinned* piece) moves, there is greater loss.

If Black falls for the trap, the moves continue as on page 38 and White ends up 2 Pawns ahead once more.

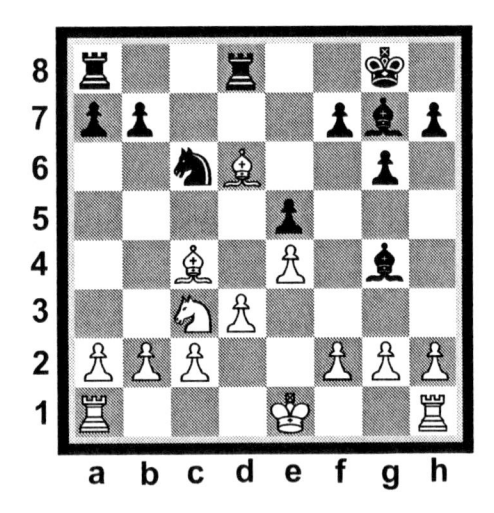

9.	BxN	BxQ
10.	BxQ	BxN
11.	Bxc7	Bg4
12.	Bxd6	Rfd8

Once again, White could end up a piece ahead, depending on Black's play. Follow these steps:

10.	BxQ	RxB
11.	PxB	

Let's look at 2 other ways Black may develop pieces and not fall into White's trap.

Case 1: Better Defense for White

7.	Bg5	Be6

The change could occur at Move 7 for Black. Rather than castling, as before, which is a good move, Black could move Be6 or Nb4.

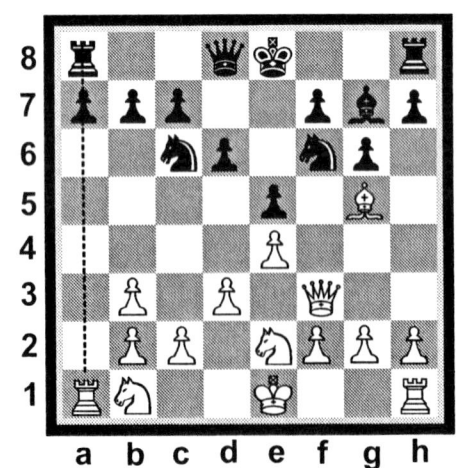

8.	Bb3	BxB
9.	PaxB	...

At Move 8, White should retreat the Bishop from c4 to b3.

Then, if in Move 8 the Black Bishop takes the White Bishop now at b3, White captures Black's Bishop with the a-Pawn (Move 9), opening up the White Rook to attack all along the a-file and maintaining a strong Pawn structure.

Note: If, on Move 8, White captures Black's Bishop at e6 (8. BxB), then Black captures White's Bishop with the f-Pawn (8. ... PxB). Black can now put the Rook at f8, a potential threat to White's Queen at f3.

Case 2: Back to Move 7 for Black

7. Bg5   Nb4

This is an attack on the unprotected Pawn at c2. If the Knight takes c2 with check then, on the next move, Black can capture the Rook at a1.

7. Bb3   ...

White's move protects the a2 and c2 Pawns, while maintaining control of the a2-a8 diagonal.

In response Black has many choices. Black could move the Bishop from c8 to d7, d6 or g4. Or, Black could choose to move the Queen from d8 to e7, perhaps planning to castle Queenside. Another possibility is to move the c-Pawn to c6 or the h-Pawn to h6.

As soon as possible, White would like to move a3 to chase the Knight away. But, depending on Black's move, White may have to delay this move. This is where players must take time to think.

Hum .... Take time to think!

Activity 8
The Queen's Raid

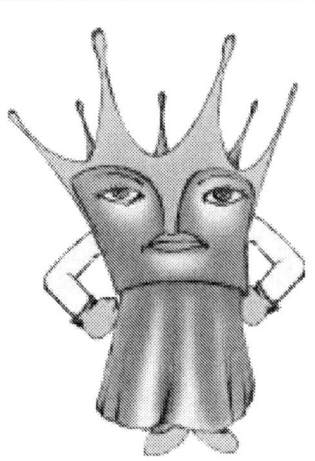

You will really understand an opening when you are able to describe it without using a chessboard. Try the following activity to help you develop this skill. This practice will also help you visualize the board if you want to play *blindfold chess*. Remember, there's always a light square in the lower right corner of the board.

Below is the list of opening moves for the Queen's Raid. Without looking at the board, use notation to fill in the score sheet correctly.
Remember! White always begins play on the 1st and 2nd ranks.

Challenge: For each piece, identify whether it has moved to a light or dark square.

Ne2   Qf3   Bc4   e4   e5   Qh5   g6   Nc6   Nf6

Queen's Raid Score Sheet

Move #	White's Moves	Challenge Light/Dark	Black's Moves	Challenge Light/Dark
1				
2				
3				
4				
5			xxxx	xxxx

Note: The opening is complete after White's 5th move.

Answer to
Activity 8, The Queen's Raid

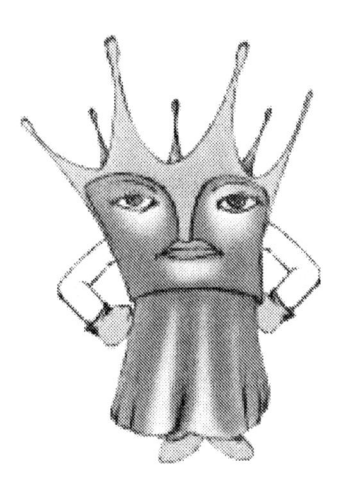

Queen's Raid Score Sheet

Move #	White's Moves	Challenge Light/Dark	Black's Moves	Challenge Light/Dark
1	e4	Light	e5	Dark
2	Qh5	Light	Nc6	Light
3	Bc4	Light	g6	Light
4	Qf3	Light	Nf6	Dark
5	Ne2	Light	xxxx	xxxx

Activity 9
The Queen's Raid

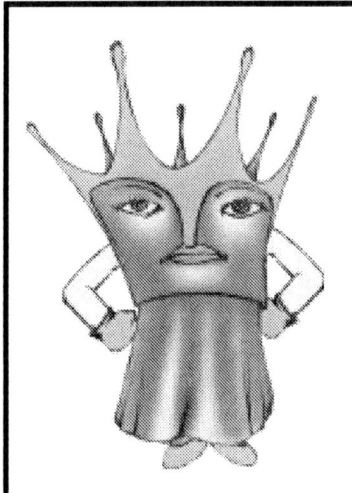

Below is the Queen's Raid played by an Expert against a computer. White's Queen is trapped on the 11th move.

Because the Expert didn't make the correct 5th move, Ne2, the computer could make the best move, 5. ... Nd4!.

If you have a computer chess program, play White. See how your computer plays against the Queen's Raid.

#	WHITE	BLACK	#	WHITE	BLACK
1	e4	e5	16		
2	Qh5	Nc6	17		
3	Bc4	g6	18		
4	Qf3	Nf6	19		
5	Qb3?	Nd4!	20		
6	Qc3	Nxe4	21		
7	Qd3	d5	22		
8	Bb5+	c6	23		
9	Ba4	Nc5	24		
10	Qa3	Nxa4	25		
11	Qxa4	b5	26		
12			27		
13			28		
14			29		
15			30		

Note: Your computer must reply e5 to your first move before you can play the Queen's Raid. You may need to choose a different level of difficulty, use *takeback move*, *force move*, or switch sides to get the computer to play the Queen's Raid. This is the only puzzle with no answer because you will be using your own computer to see the results.

Activity 10
The Queen's Raid Puzzles 1 & 2

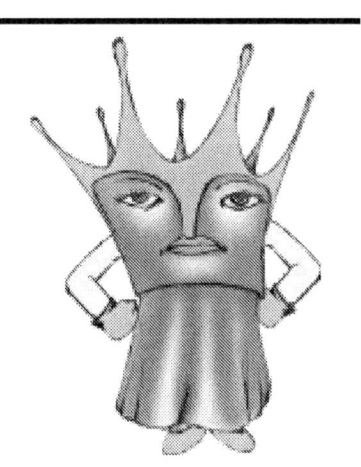

Work these puzzles to learn more about the Queen's Raid.

Puzzle 1

Many players plan to start the Queen's Raid by bringing the Bishop out on the second move. This makes it easy for Black to stop the raid.

What is Black's best move? _____

Puzzle 2

Another mistake White often makes when attempting the Queen's Raid: moving the Queen to h3 instead of f3 on the 4th move.

What is Black's best move? _____

Answers to Activity 10
The Queen's Raid Puzzles 1 & 2

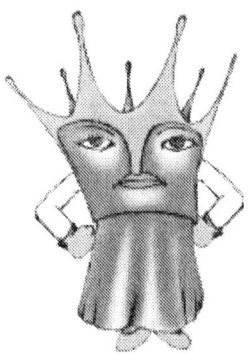

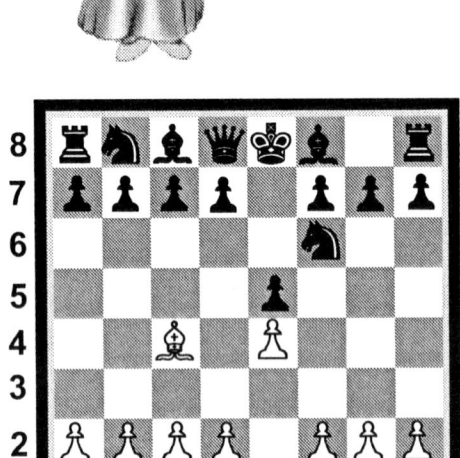

Puzzle 1

Answer: Nf6 prevents White's Queen from moving to h5. If you're going to play the Queen's Raid, always bring your Queen out on the second move.

Note: If White brings the Bishop out on the second move, it's called the **Bishop's Opening**.

Puzzle 2

Answer: d5 allows Black to attack White twice: the Pawn at d5 attacks White's Bishop and Black's Bishop (c8) has a *discovered attack* on White's Queen.

Often, White will notice only the attack on the Bishop because the Pawn moved. White fails to see the *discovered attack* on the Queen. Even if White sees the *discovered attack* and saves the Queen, White will still lose the Bishop.

A *discovered attack* occurs when one piece moves, exposing an attack by the piece it once blocked. The attacking piece does not move.

Activity 11
The Queen's Raid Puzzles 3 & 4

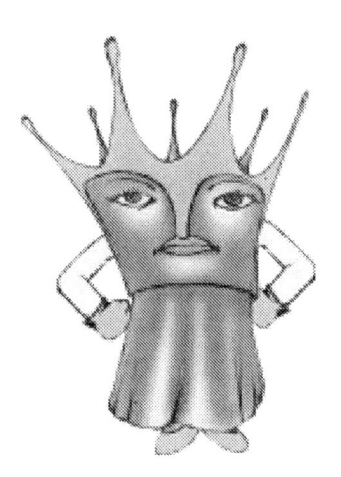

Puzzle 3

On White's previous move, the White Bishop moved to g5, attacking Black's Knight at f6. Then, Black brought the Bishop out, attacking White's Queen at f3.

What is White's best move? _____

Puzzle 4

Many times White will try unwise attacks to carry out the original plan for the Queen's Raid. Here, White wants to move a Pawn to g5 to chase the Black Knight away from f6 and open f7 for capture and checkmate.

What is Black's best move? _____

Answers to Activity 11
The Queen's Raid Puzzles 3 & 4

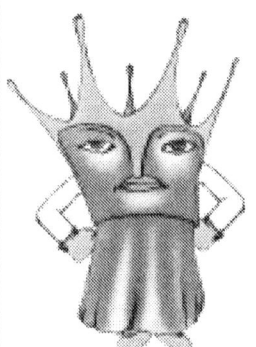

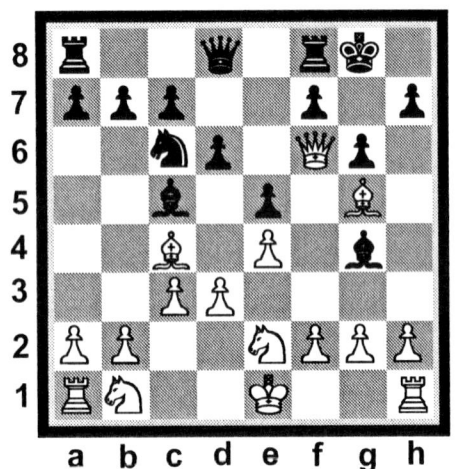

Puzzle 3

Answer: **QxN** allows White to gain a free Knight. In Black's haste to attack White's Queen, Black did not notice that the Knight was under double attack by the Queen and the Bishop. Black should have moved the King to *g7*, which is the only way to protect the Knight.

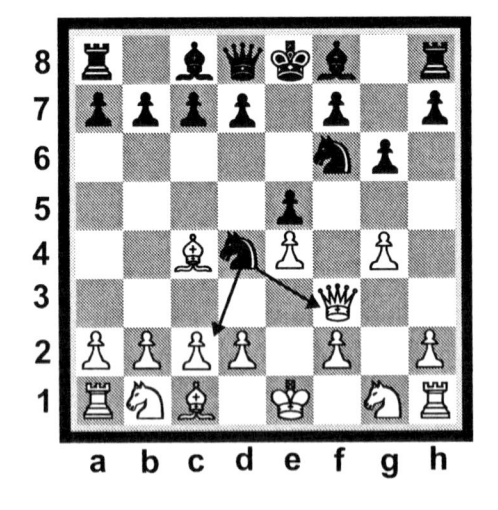

Puzzle 4

Answer: Black stops the Queen's Raid with **Nd4** and starts the attack. This move — a Knight's *fork* — attacks White's Queen and the unprotected Pawn at *c2*. Now, the White Queen cannot stay on the f-file. Black is no longer threatened with checkmate by White.

If Black can take *c2*, it will *fork* White's King and Rook.

A *fork* occurs when one piece simultaneously attacks 2 pieces.

Activity 12
The Queen's Raid, Fork Puzzle 1

In the Queen's Raid, as in most chess openings, there's the threat of a *fork,* attacking at least 2 of your opponent's pieces with only one of yours.

The Knight is easy to use, even in the opening when many pieces are blocked. The Knight can't be blocked and it can create tricky combinations. One of its most exciting moves is when it attacks its opponent's Queen and King at the same time.

Hint: They must be on the same color squares. You may need to sac (sacrifice) a piece to set up the fork.

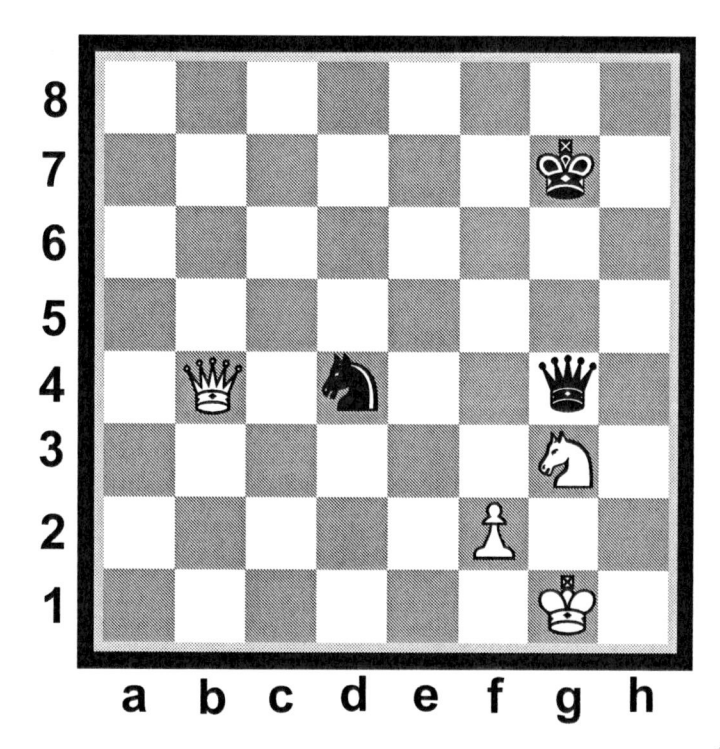

White to move: White can *fork* Black's King and Queen in only 2 moves.

1. What is White's first move? _____

2. What must Black do next? _____

3. How does White set the *fork*? _____

Note: The Knight at g3 is *pinned* and cannot move.

Can you figure out this puzzle?

Copyright © 2002, 2005 Teachable Tech, Inc.
All Rights Reserved.

Chapter 4
The Queen's Raid Activities

Answers to Activity 12
The Queen's Raid, Fork Puzzle 1

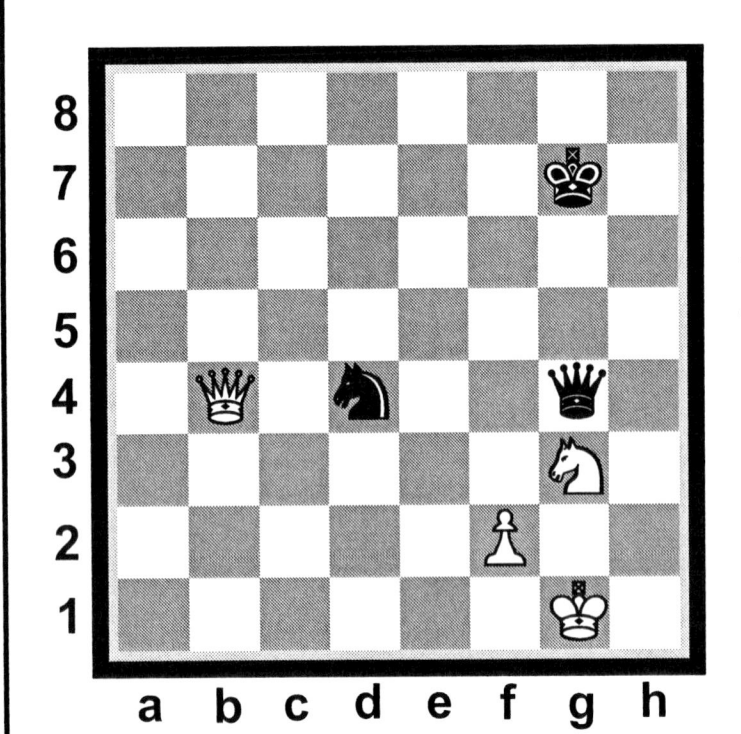

1. White: QxN+
2. Black: QxQ
3. White: Nf5+

Note: With QxN+, White forces Black to take the Queen to get out of check, removing the *pin*⭐ on the White Knight. This allows the White Knight to move away from his King and set the *fork* on Black's King and Queen, a winning advantage.

⭐ For more on pins, see Chapter 9, The Power of the Pin (page 107).

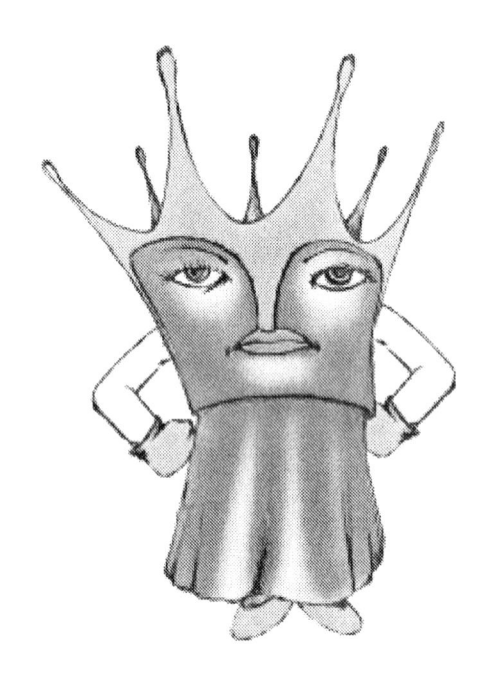

Activity 13
The Queen's Raid, Fork Puzzle 2

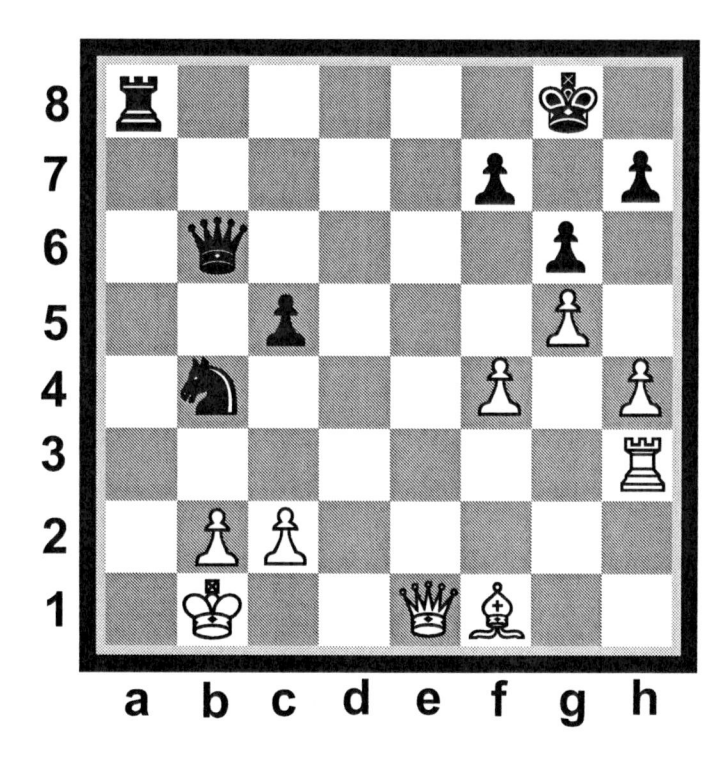

Black to move: Black can fork White's King and Queen in 2 moves: the first move prepares for the fork and the second sets the fork.

What does Black do first? _____

How is White forced to reply? _____

What's Black's move to set the fork? _____

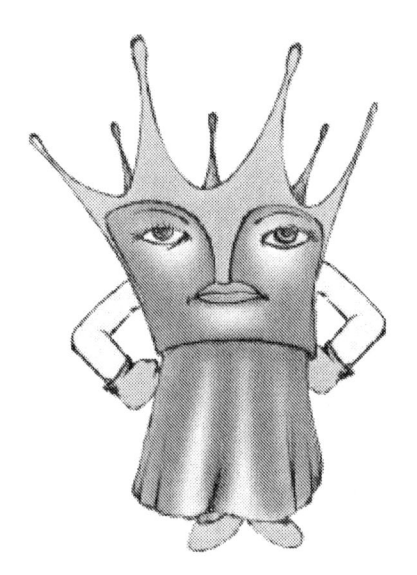

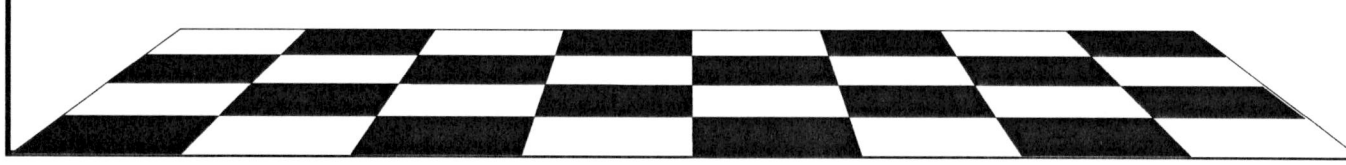

Answers to Activity 13
The Queen's Raid, Fork Puzzle 2

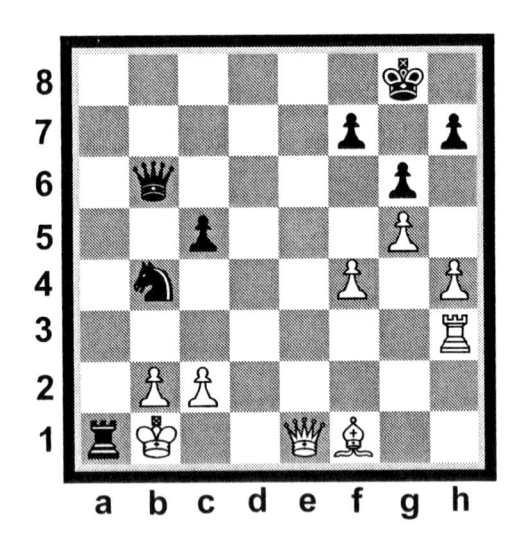

1. ...   Ra1+

Black moves its Rook to a1 with check. White's King has only one move.

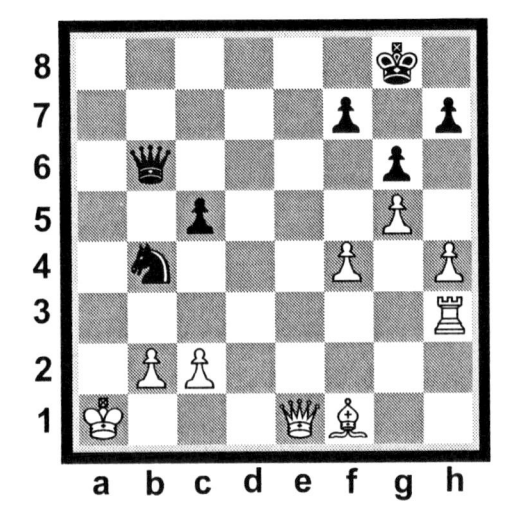

2. KxR

The board is ready for Black to set the fork.

2. ...   Nxc2+

Both the King and Queen are attacked. On White's next move, the King must escape check.

3. Ka2 or b1   NxQ

Black loses the Rook but gains the Queen and Pawn. This material advantage should win the game for Black.

Activity 14
The Queen's Raid, Fork Puzzle 3

It takes White 3 steps to set the fork. What are the moves? What are Black's responses?

1. _____ _____

2. _____ _____

3. _____ _____

4. _____ any K move

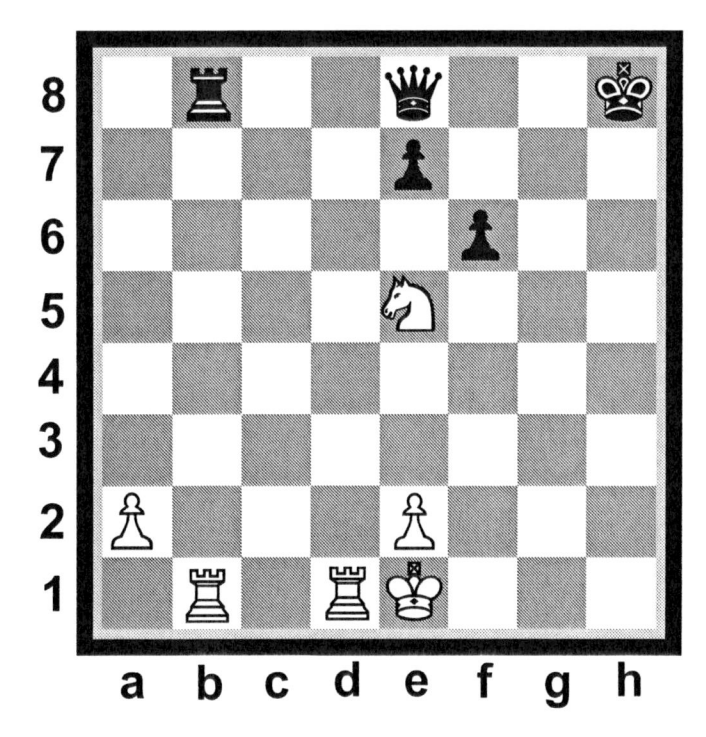

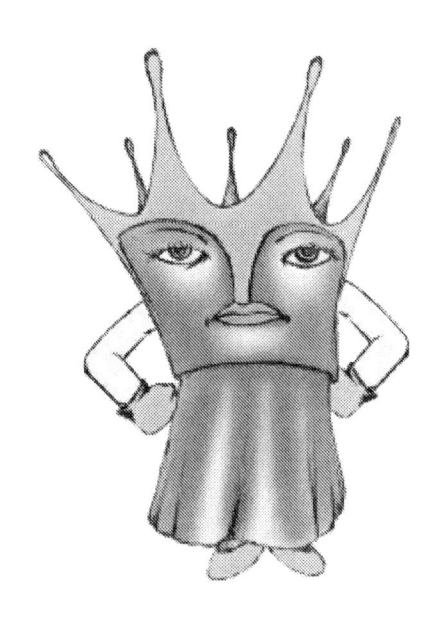

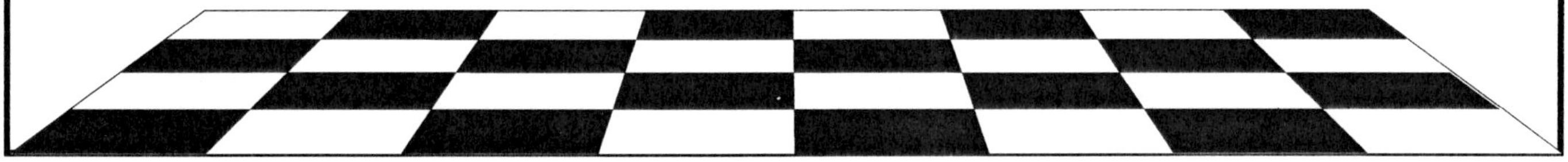

Answers to
Activity 14
The Queen's Raid, Fork Puzzle 3

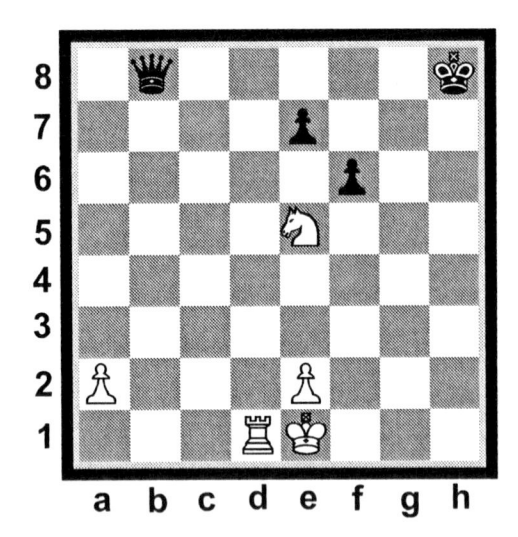

1. RxR   QxR

When White takes Black's Rook at b8, the Black Queen is forced to take White's Rook.

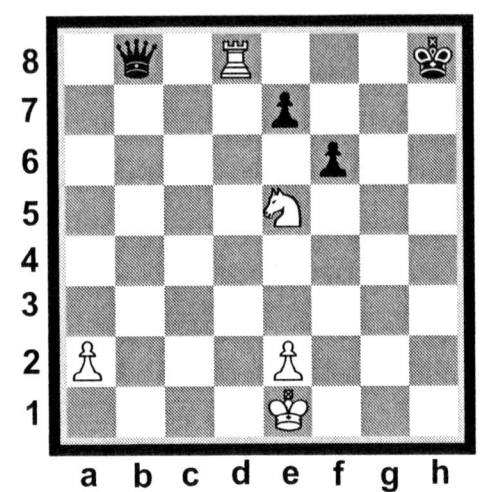

2. Rd8+   QxR

Black has no choice but to take White's Rook at d8.

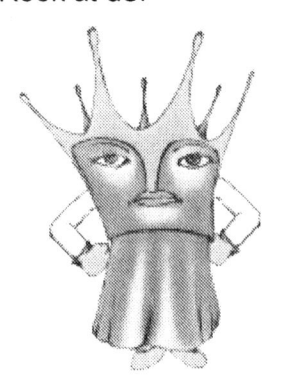

3. Nf7+   any K move

Here's the KQ Knight Fork. The King is in check and the Knight can't be blocked so the King must move. Black loses the Queen and White has an easy win because of the *passed Pawn* at a2.

4. NxQ!

A *passed Pawn* has no Pawns that can stop its advance.

Activity 15
The Queen's Raid, Fork Puzzle 4

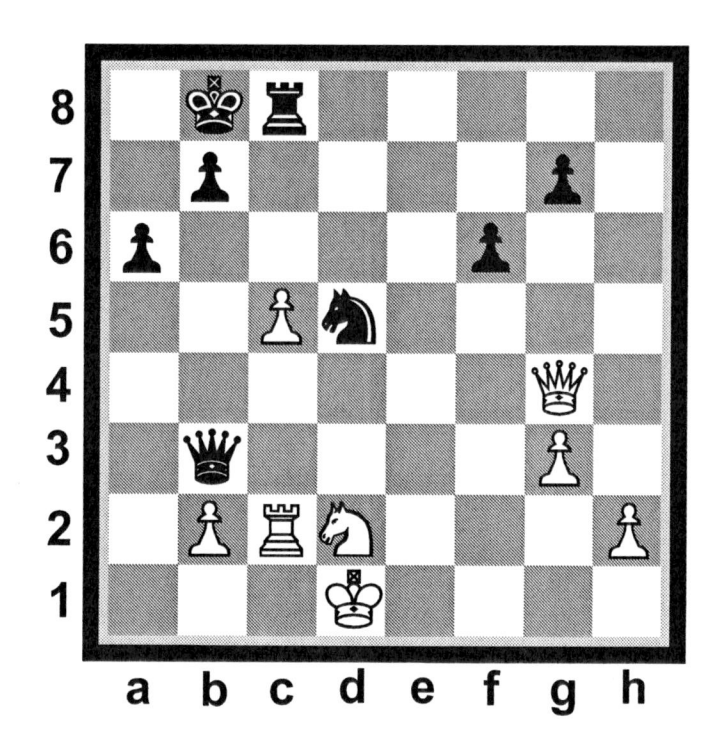

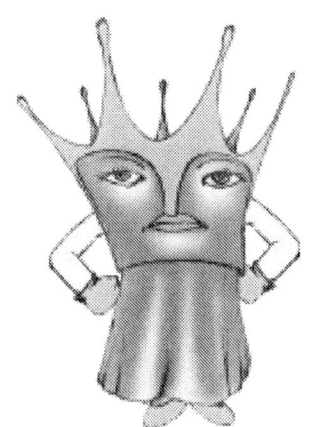

Black to move:

Black can set a *fork* in just 1 move.

1. What is Black's move? _____

2. Is this the best move for Black? Why or why not? _____
_____

Black can set a *fork* on White's King and Queen in 2 moves.

1. What is Black's first move? _____

2. What must White do next? _____

3. How does Black set the *fork*? _____

4. Why is this a better move? _____

Chapter 4
The Queen's Raid Activities

Answers to
Activity 15, The Queen's Raid, Fork Puzzle 4

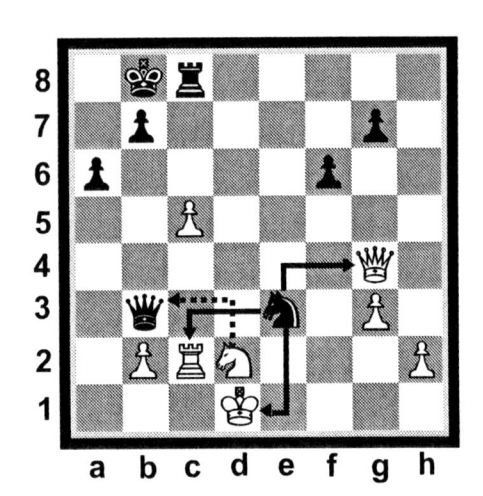

1. ... Ne3+

1. With this move, Black *forks* White's Queen at g4, White's Rook at c2 and White's King at d1.

2. This is an advantage for Black, but not as big an advantage as it may seem. Look again... White's Knight at d2 is attacking Black's Queen. In this case, White and Black are just trading Queens with no material advantage for Black.

Follow these moves to see a better plan for Black.

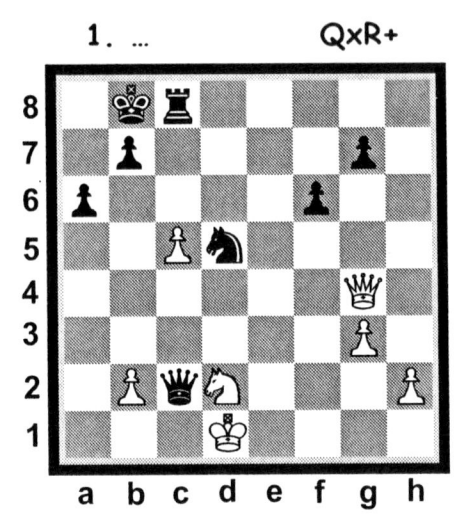

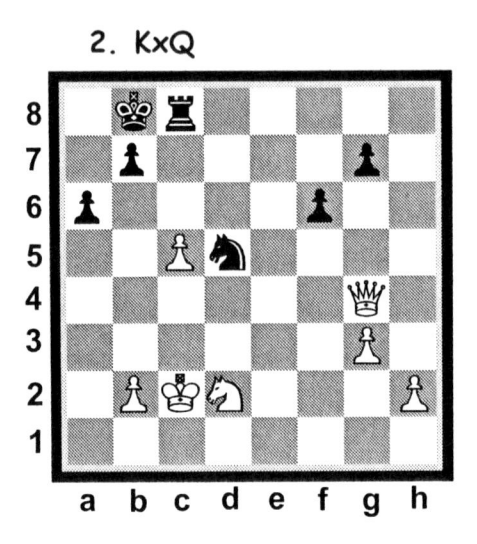

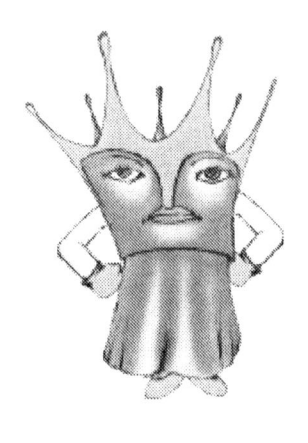

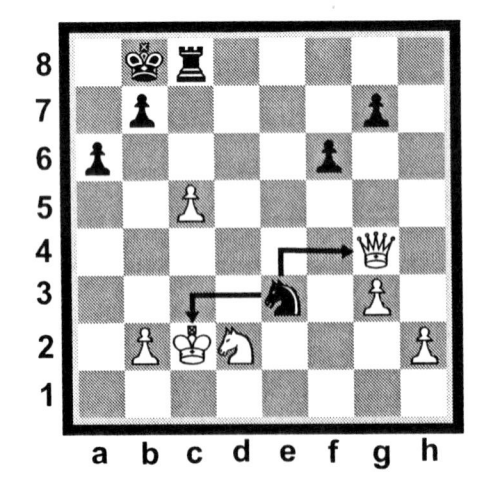

1. ... QxR+

2. KxQ

2. ... Ne3+

Black *forks* White's King and Queen. When the King is part of the *fork* and the Knight cannot be captured, the King must move. White has gained a Queen and Rook, while giving up only a Queen.

Chapter 5
En Passant

Remember, *En Passant* can happen:

1. **only** between 2 Pawns;
2. **only** if a Pawn moves 2 spaces;
3. **only** if an opponent's Pawn is on the adjacent file; and,
4. **only** if the capture takes place immediately following the Pawn's move.

Don't remember En Passant?

Read page 23 in **Chapter 3: Chess Notation, Capturing and Special Moves** to refresh your memory before working this puzzle.

En Passant means "in passing."

Activity 16

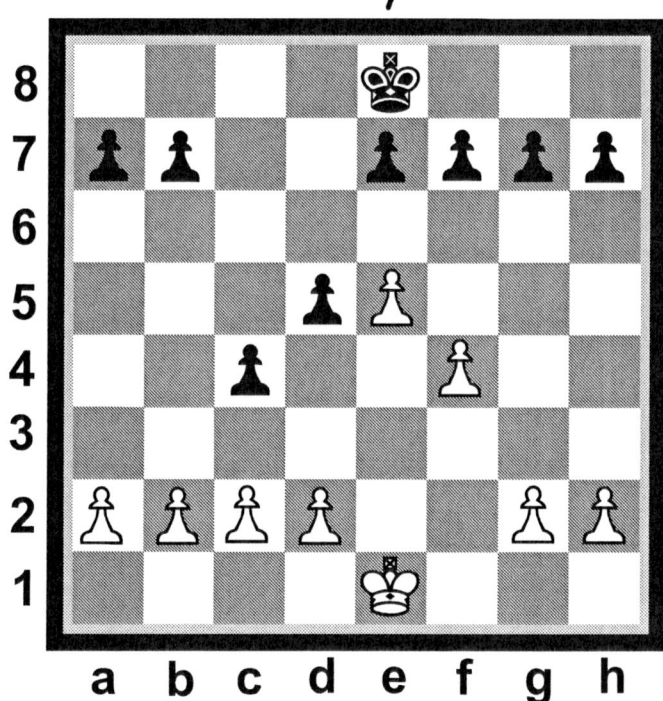

From this position, circle the Black and White Pawns that, if moved 2 spaces, could be captured *en passant*.

Draw an arrow to show where the captor moves. Find all 3 of the possibilities.

Challenge: Write the notation for both Black and White moves *en passant*.

Answers to Activity 16 En Passant

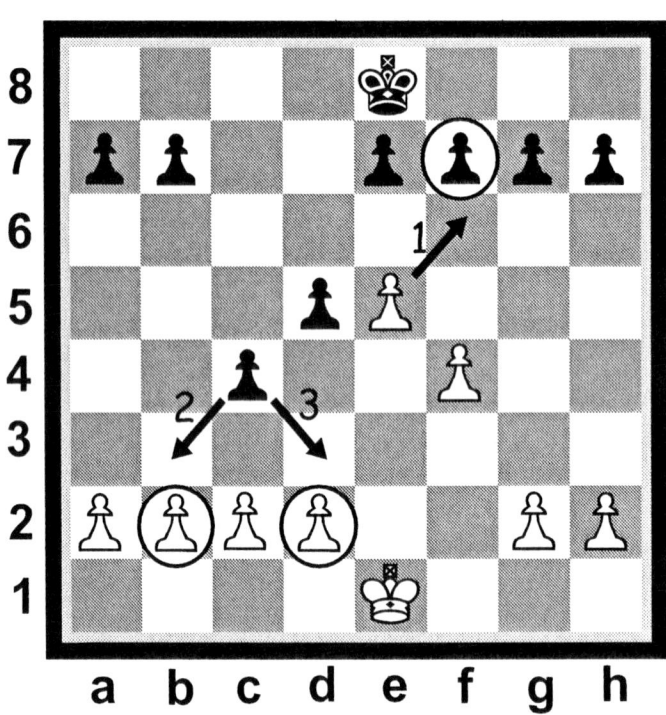

Challenge:

White	Black
1. ...	f5
ef e.p.	

White	Black
2. b4	cb e.p.

White	Black
3. d4	cd e.p.

Chapter 6a
Two Knights Defense, Part 1

The **Two Knights Defense**, more properly called the **Chigorin Counterattack**, is one of the first openings and it is played at all levels. We recommend this strategy for the scholastic player. It is good for both Black and White. Usually, this is an *open game*: pawns trade in the center, leaving open and half-open files for rapid movement of pieces and exciting attacks. This opening, like the Queen's Raid, has many traps.

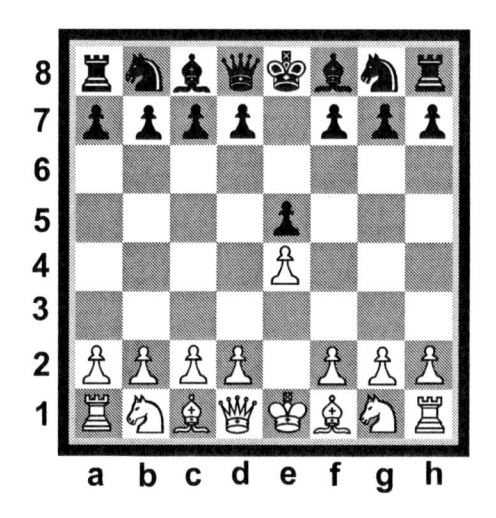

1. e4   e5

The most powerful opening for the beginning scholastic player is e4 for White and e5 in response. (See *Queen's Raid*.)

With this move, both Black and White compete for control of the center. Players prepare for rapid development of pieces.

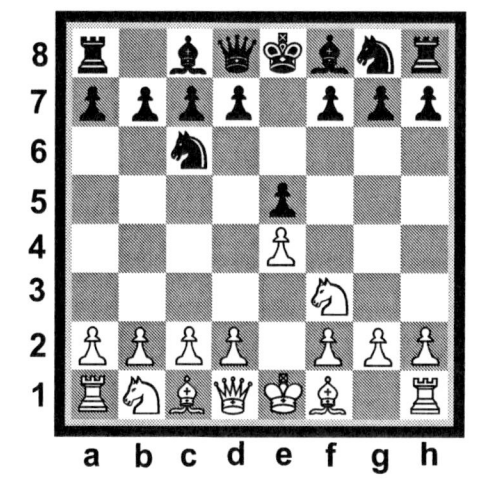

2. Nf3   Nc6

White's second move — Knight to f3, attacking Black's Pawn at e5 — makes this opening very similar to the Queen's Raid, where the Queen comes out attacking e5.

Black's response is the same as in the Queen's Raid: Knight to c6. This develops a piece and protects the Pawn at e5.

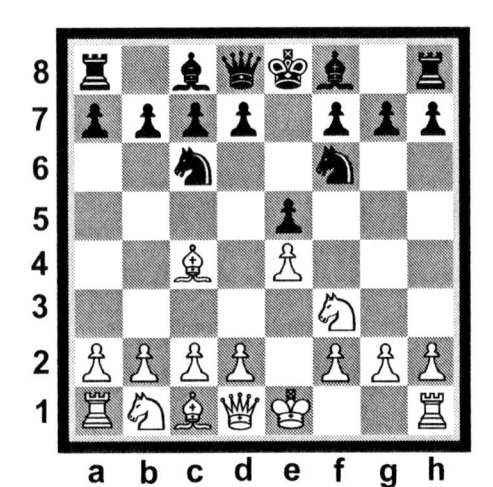

3. Bc4   Nf6

White's third move, Bishop to c4, indicates that White is playing a style of opening called the **Italian Game**. This developing move helps White maintain the opening advantage, as now White is ready to castle. The move also helps White control the center by preventing Black's Pawn from moving safely to d5. White's Bishop also attacks the f7 Pawn, protected only by the King.

For Black to continue to follow the 3 principles of openings, Black must either develop the Kingside Bishop or Knight. In the Two Knight's Defense, Black brings out the Knight to f6, attacking White's unprotected Pawn at e4, putting pressure on d5. The Two Knights Defense could be called the "Two Knights Attack."

4. Ng5

White's move, Ng5, attacks and defends at the same time. It creates a *double attack* on the Pawn at f7, similar to the attack in the Queen's Raid, while protecting the Pawn at e4. Unlike the Queen's Raid, White's Queen is still at d1. White has developed 2 minor pieces and is ready to castle.

Note: Usually you move each piece only once in the opening to develop pieces rapidly and fight for control of the center. But, in this case, to get the *double attack* on f7, we had to move our Knight twice.

4. ...   d5

Black can't protect the Pawn at f7 but can block the attack. Black can't block the Knight because it can jump; but, by moving the Pawn to d5, Black blocks the White Bishop's attack.

This move also allows Black to develop the Queenside Bishop that is often blocked at c8.

5. ed (PxP)

Pawn takes Pawn keeps White's attack going. If Bishop takes Pawn, half of White's attack will be ended because Black's Knight can take the Bishop.

5. ...   Na5

Black does not capture the Pawn d5 — that would *pin* the Knight. If the Knight were to move, the double attack on f7 by the White Bishop and Knight would be restored.

So, if the Knight at f6 doesn't capture the Pawn, the Knight at c6 must move or be captured. Black's plan to move the Knight to a5, attacking White's Bishop, is to force the Bishop off the a2 to g8 diagonal and stop the double attack on f7.

Note: Often, players say, "Knights on the rim are grim." Here, it's so important to stop the attack that we recommend the move to a5, even though it puts the Knight on the rim and is its second move in the opening.

White has an extra Pawn here, but Black has greater development and is now attacking. Therefore, the position is considered even.

This is not the end of the opening. There are more moves to be covered in Chapter 6b.

Work through the following activities and puzzles in the Two Knights Defense.

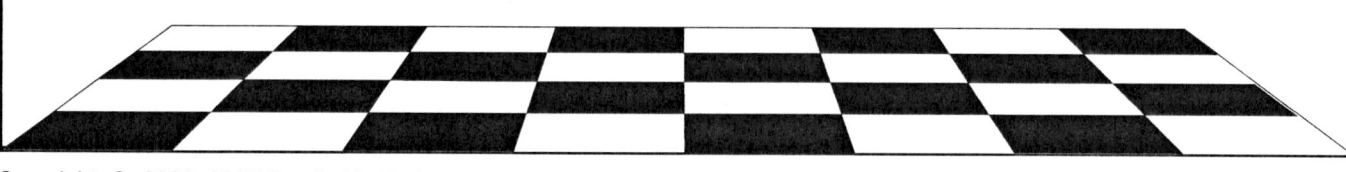

Activity 17
Two Knights Defense, Part 1

If you really understand an opening, you should be able to describe it without using a chessboard. Try the following activity to help you develop this skill. This practice will also help you visualize the board if you want to play *blindfold chess*.

On the score sheet below, fill in the first 5 moves for White and Black in the Two Knights Defense from memory, without looking at a board.

Two Knights Defense Score Sheet

#	White	Black	#	White	Black
1			15		
2			16		
3			17		
4			18		
5			19		

Now, fill in the board below to show the position after the fifth move. Use letters to show the pieces. Use W for White and B for Black.

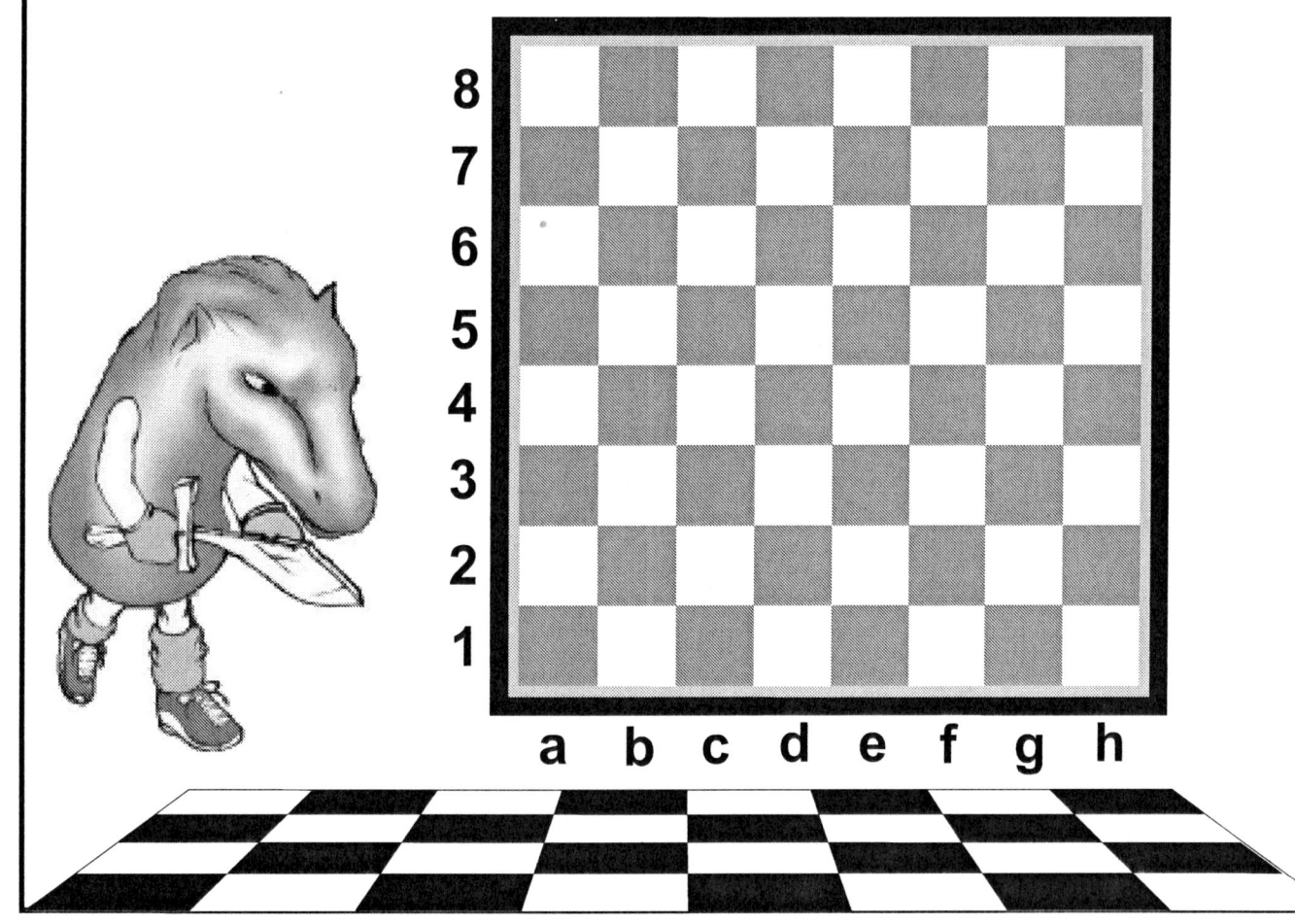

Answer to
Activity 17: Two Knights Defense, Part 1

Two Knights Defense Score Sheet

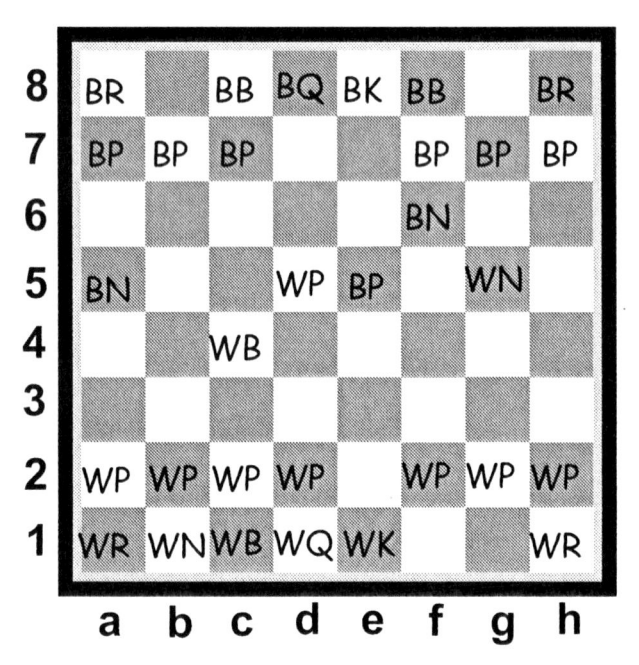

#	White	Black	#	White	Black
1	e4	e5	15		
2	Nf3	Nc6	16		
3	Bc4	Nf6	17		
4	Ng5	d5	18		
5	ed (PxP)	Na5	19		

Chapter 6a
Two Knights Defense, Part 1 Activities

Activity 18
Two Knights Defense, Part 1
Puzzles 1 & 2

Puzzle 1

In the Two Knights Defense, both sides are fighting for control of the center, rapidly developing pieces and preparing to castle early.

1. So, what's wrong with this picture if you're playing the Two Knights Defense?

   _____

2. What is the correct move for Black?

   _____

Note: Black's second move Nf6, is called Petroff's Defense.

Puzzle 2

Move 4, Nc3, is a slightly inferior move often made by White. It does develop a piece and protect the Pawn, but it does not attack. A better move would be Ng5.

What is Black's best move?

Answers to
Activity 18, The 2 Knights Defense, Part 1
Puzzles 1 & 2

Puzzle 1

1. In the Two Knights Defense, Black moves (2. ... Nc6) to protect the Pawn at e5, before attacking White's Pawn at e4.

   White has the advantage of the first move, so Black needs to try to equalize before attempting to attack. White can capture first. Black should protect its Pawn (2. ... Nc6) rather than attack White's Pawn.

2. Correct move: Nc6

Puzzle 2

Nxe4, the *fork trick*. At first, the move looks like Black is giving up the Knight for a Pawn. When the White Knight at c3 captures the Black Knight at e4, the board is set for Black to *fork* the Knight at e4 and the Bishop at c4. So, with Black's move to d5, Black regains the piece and takes the initiative. White can save only one of the forked pieces. There is more on this in Chapter 7.

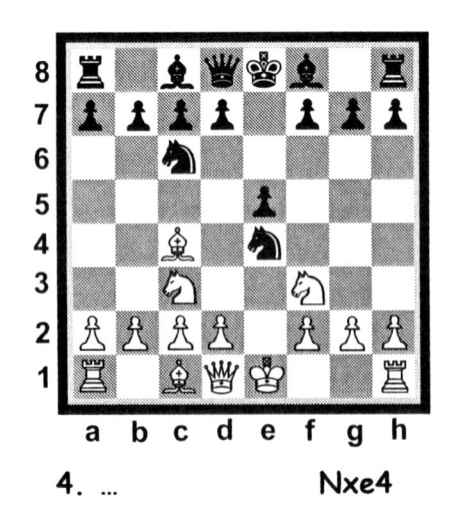

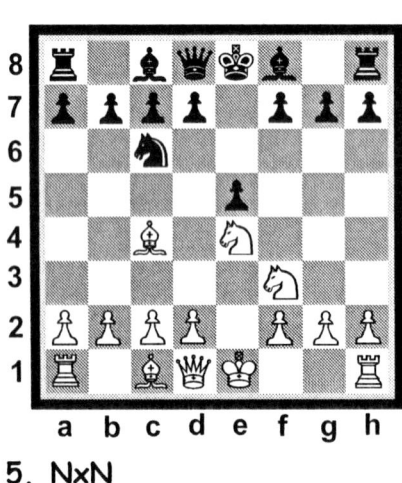

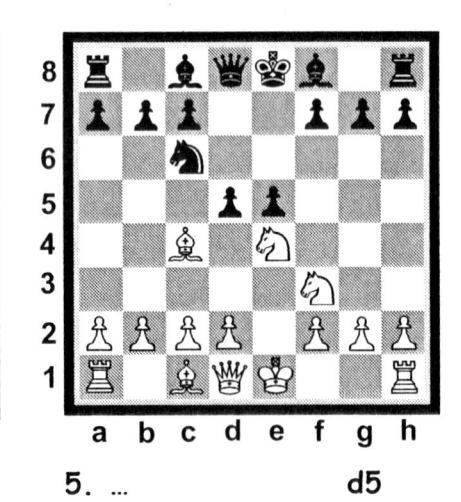

4. ...   Nxe4   5. NxN   5. ...   d5

Copyright © 2002, 2005 Teachable Tech, Inc.
All Rights Reserved.

Chapter 6a
Two Knights Defense, Part 1 Activities

Chapter 6b
Two Knights Defense, Part 2

Now, you're ready to complete the Two Knights Defense. This is where we stopped in the previous chapter.

1. e4	e5
2. Nf3	Nc6
3. Bc4	Nf6
4. Ng5	d5
5. ed (PxP)	Na5

On the 5th move, Black's Knight goes to a5, trying to move the White Bishop off the a2 to g8 diagonal.

Note: If Black's Knight goes to d4 instead, Black is playing the **Fritz Variation** of the *Two Knights Defense*. (See a sample game in the answer to Activity 19, page 74.)

| 6. Bb5+ | c6 |

The White Bishop moves to b5 and attacks the King with check.

To escape check, usually, first try to capture, next to block and finally to flee. Here, Black can't capture, but can block with either the Pawn or the Bishop. The better move for the scholastic player is using the Pawn to block at c6. It is more forceful.

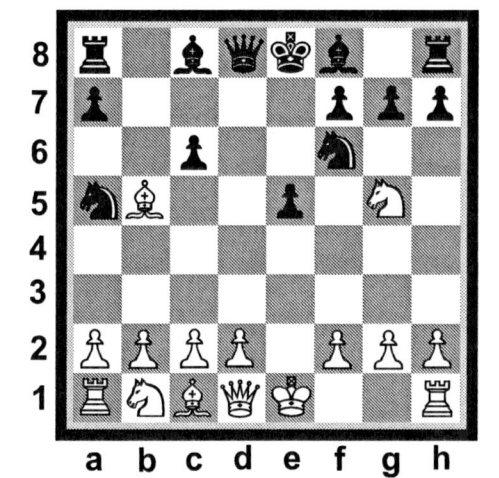

| 7. dc (PxP) | bc (PxP) |

There's not much change on the board with this trade. But, White has traded the doubled d-Pawn, improved Pawn structure and weakened Black's Pawns. Black still has a Pawn attacking White's Bishop.

8. Be2　　　　　　　　　　h6

Moving back to e2 is the best move for White's Bishop.

In the opening, players should be wary of moving the f-, g- or h-Pawns. In this case, Black decides to continue the attack and gains space with the Pawn move to h6.

9. Nf3　　　　　　　　　　e4

White is retreating.

Black continues the attack. Black takes more space and moves the e-Pawn forward, where it no longer attacks a center square, but attacks White's Knight.

White is up a Pawn after the 9th move. But, look at White's lack of development. Neither side has castled yet.

10. Ne5　　　　　　　　　Bd6

White's undefended Knight attempts to stay in the center, but is only attacked once more as Black develops the Bishop and prepares to castle.

Keep going! There are only 4 more moves in this most popular line of the Two Knights Defense.

11. d4   **ed e.p. (PxP e.p.)**

White tries to defend the Knight in the center by moving the Pawn to d4.

Black *removes the defender by capturing d4 en passant* and continues the attack on the now undefended Knight with the Bishop. Simultaneously, Black's Pawn at d3 attacks White's Bishop at e2.

Note: See page 142 and The Basics for more information on *en passant*.

12. Nxd3

White has been able to hold the position with a Pawn advantage.

Black has more space and better development. This position is still considered equal.

12. ...   **Qc7**

Black's move prevents White from castling. If White castles now, then the Black Bishop takes the Pawn at h2 with check.

Note: The Queen at c7 and the Bishop at d6 form a *battery,* attacking White's Pawn at h2.

> *A battery* is the doubling of forces, such as when a Queen and Bishop, Rook and Rook, or Queen and Rook are lined up together to strengthen the power of an attack.

13. f4   0-0

White's move to f4 blocks Black's *battery* so that White will be able to castle on the next move.

Black now castles to get his King to safety to be ready to attack.

14. 0-0   c5

White is finally able to castle, still maintaining a Pawn advantage.

Black's move to c5 allows a quick way for the Black Knight to get back in the game. Black is ready to begin an all-out attack and has a great advantage in development.

This is the end of the main line of the *Two Knight's Defense*. We're now ready to begin the **middle game**. A sharp, tactical player will have the advantage with Black; a strong positional player will have the advantage with White. Practice playing many games from this position.

A positional player is one who prefers closed games to give them time to exploit small advantages to consolidate a winning position.

A tactical player is one who prefers open games and uses traps, threats and plans based on combinations or variations to establish a winning position; often, called a gambit player.

Which kind of player are you: sharp and tactical or strong and positional?

Activity 19
Two Knights Defense, Part 2

If you really understand an opening, you should be able to describe it without using a chessboard. Try the following visual activity to help you develop this skill. This practice will also help you visualize the board if you want to play *blindfold chess*.

Below is the list of opening moves for the complete Two Knights Defense. Without looking at the board, use the notation to fill in the score sheet correctly.

Hint: Use a pencil to cross out each move below as you write it on the notation grid.

Bb5+	Bc4	Bd6	Be2	bc	c5	c6
d4	d5	dc	0-0	e4	0-0	ed
ed e.p.	f4	h6	Na5	Nc6	Nf3	Nf3
Ne5	Nf6	Ng5	Nxd3	Qc7		

Challenge: For each piece try to identify whether it has moved to a light or dark square.

#	White	Black	#	White	Black
1	e4	e5	8		
2			9		
3			10		
4			11		
5			12		
6			13		
7			14		

The Fritz Variation: Openings have many variations. One such variation of the *Two Knights Defense* is the Fritz Variation. Look at this variation notated on the next page.

Answer to
Activity 19, Two Knights Defense, Part 2

#	White	Black	#	White	Black
1	e4 (Light)	e5 (Dark)	8	Be2 (Light)	h6 (Dark)
2	Nf3 (Light)	Nc6 (Light)	9	Nf3 (Light)	e4 (Light)
3	Bc4 (Light)	Nf6 (Dark)	10	Ne5 (Dark)	Bd6 (Dark)
4	Ng5 (Dark)	d5 (Light)	11	d4 (Dark)	ed e.p. (PxP e.p.) (Light)
5	ed (PxP) (Light)	Na5 (Dark)	12	Nxe3 (Light)	Qc7 (Dark)
6	Bb5+ (Light)	c6 (Light)	13	f4 (Dark)	0-0 (xx)
7	dc (PxP) (Light)	bc (PxP) (Light)	14	0-0 (xx)	c5 (Dark)

The Two Knights Defense, Fritz Variation Sample Game

Many players fall into a trap on move 6 by trying to continue the attack by the Bishop and Knight on f7. Follow these moves on a board and you'll see how this trap in the Fritz Variation leads to checkmate for Black in just 10 moves.

#	White	Black	#	White	Black
1	e4	e5	6	d6?	Qxd6
2	Nf3	Nc6	7	Nxf7?	Qc6
3	Bc4	Nf6	8	NxR?	Qxg2
4	Ng5	d5	9	Rf1	Qe4+
5	ed (PxP)	Nd4	10	Be2?	Nf3#

Note: Many beginning players achieve a great deal of success with this variation.

Activity 20
Two Knights Defense, Part 2
Puzzles 1 & 2

Puzzle 1

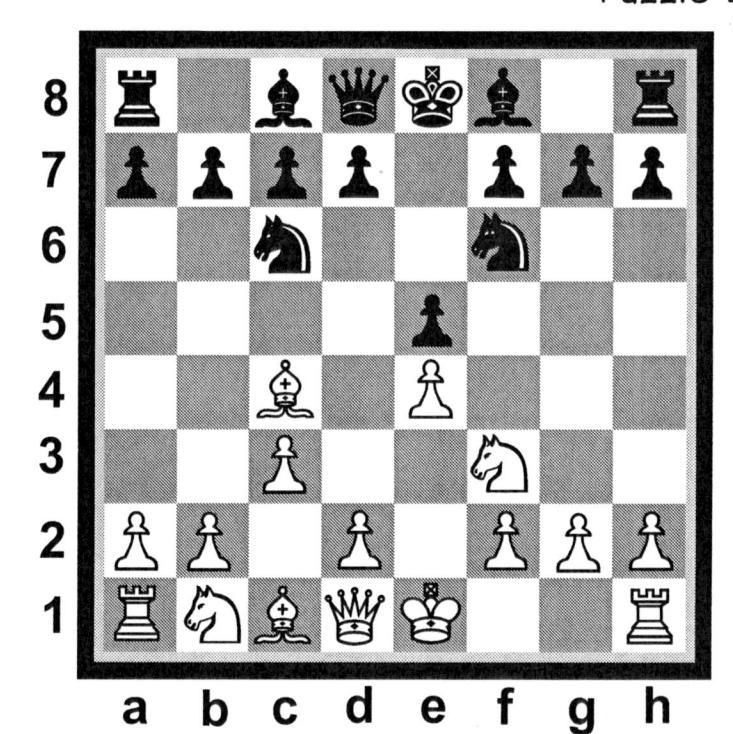

1.	e4	e5
2.	Nf3	Nc6
3.	Bc4	Nf6
4.	c3	

White moves the pawn to c3. White should have chosen one of the correct responses to the *Two Knights Defense*: move the Knight to g5 or castle.

What is Black's best move?

Puzzle 2

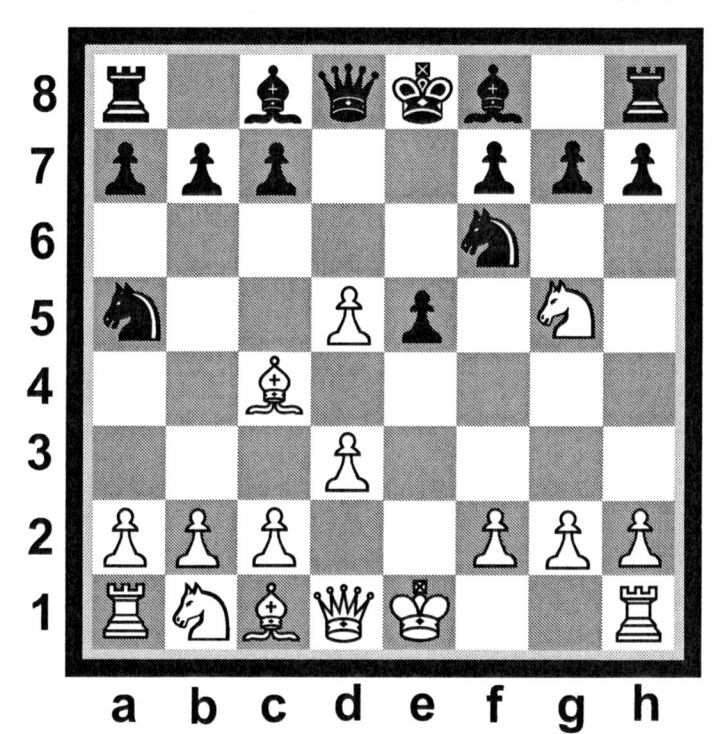

On move 6, White might move d3 to protect the Bishop at c4, rather than move the Bishop to b5.

What is Black's best move?

Answer to
Activity 20, Two Knights Defense, Part 2

Puzzle 1

4. ...   Nxe4

Black capturess the Pawn

Note: White has confused the openings. White is playing the *Giuoco Piano*, even though Black has turned the opening into the *Two Knights Defense*.

Puzzle 2

For the Beginning Player

6. d3?!   NxB

Move Black's Knight off the side of the board and eliminate White's Bishop. Black wants to move the White Bishop off the a2-g8 diagonal.

For the Advanced Player

6. d3?!   h6

This quiet move, attacking White's Knight, is very powerful. It leads to:

7. Nf3   e4

Now, White's Knight has retreated; Black's Pawn at e4 is attacking both White's Knight at f3 and the Pawn at d3. And, the Black Knight at a5 is attacking the White Bishop at c4. Try this move on your own board to see its power.

Activity 21
Two Knights Defense, Part 2
Puzzle 3

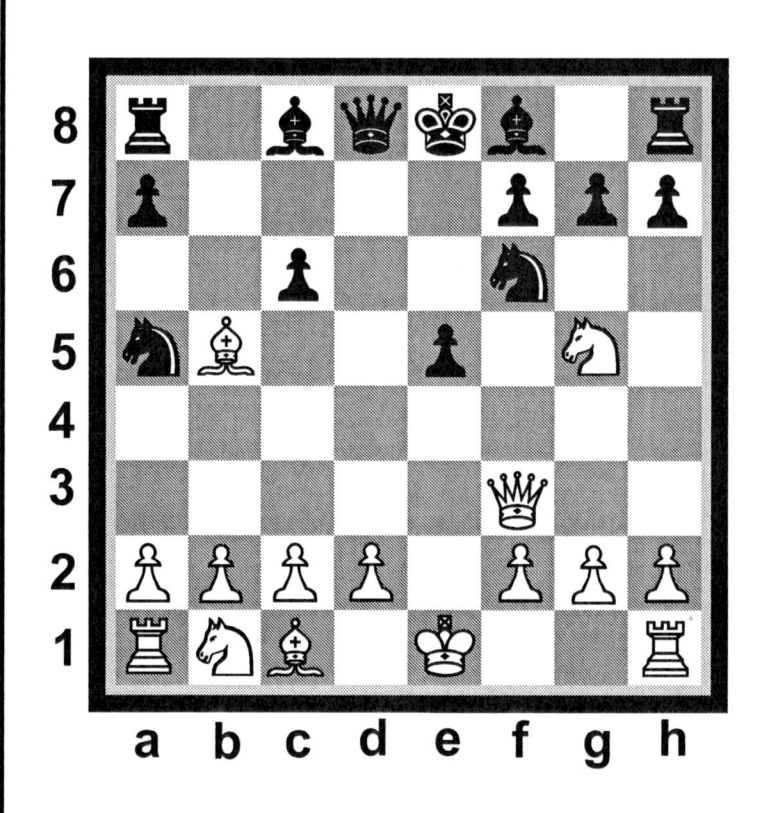

White's correct move 8 is Be2. Instead, White moves 8. Qf3, developing the Queen, attacking the pawn at c6 and *pinning* the pawn to the Rook at a8.

What is Black's best move 8?

REMEMBER the first 7 moves of the Two Knights Defense:

#	White	Black	#	White	Black
1	e4	e5	6	Bb5+	c6
2	Nf3	Nc6	7	dc (PxP)	bc (PxP)
3	Bc4	Nf6	8	Qf3!?	
4	Ng5	d5	9		
5	ed (PxP)	Na5	10		

Answer to
Activity 21, Two Knights Defense, Part 2
Puzzle 3

8. Qf3!? **Rb8**

Black's Move: Rb8 removes the *pin* and attacks the Bishop.

Then the following moves may occur:

9. Bxc6+ **NxB**

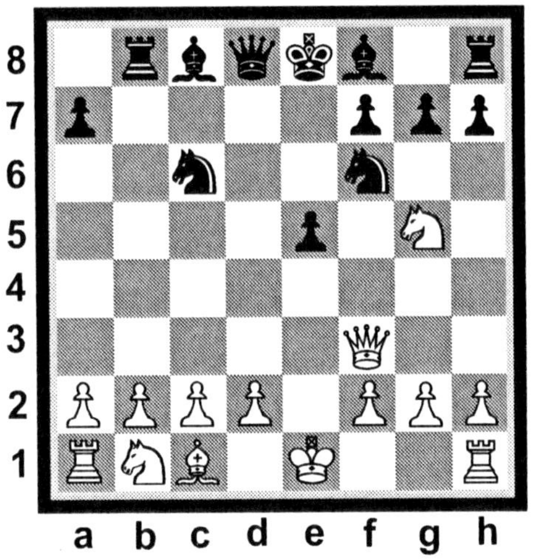

If White's Bishop takes the Pawn at c6 with check, the Black Knight takes the Bishop at c6.

10. QxN+ **Nd7**

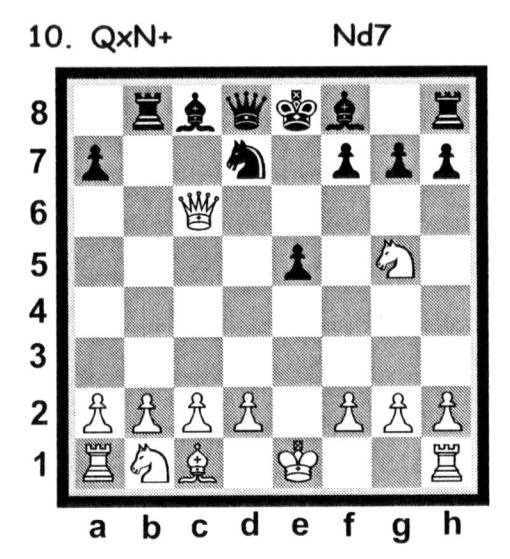

The White Queen then takes the Knight at c6 with check. Black blocks the check by moving the Knight to d7, creating a discovered attack by the Black Queen on the White Knight at g5.

Note: The move Nd7 is a better move than Bd2 because you will need the Bishop to control the a8-h1 diagonal.

White has to save the Knight. If White moves the Pawn to d3, then the Bishop at c1 is protecting the Knight. Black's threat on the next move is to move the Bishop to b7 attacking both the Queen and the Pawn at g7. This is another excellent point from which to start to practice playing, using a clock for both Black and White.

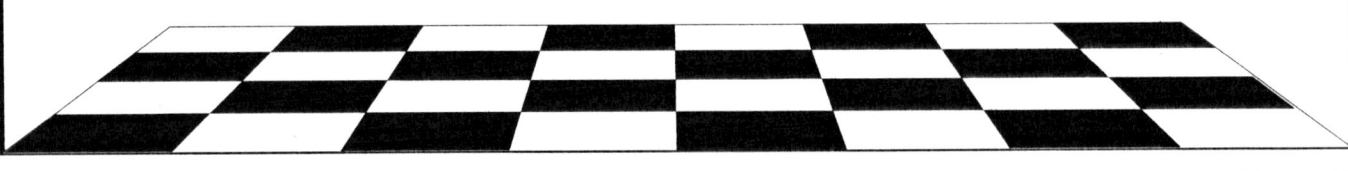

Activity 22
Two Knights Defense
Puzzle 4

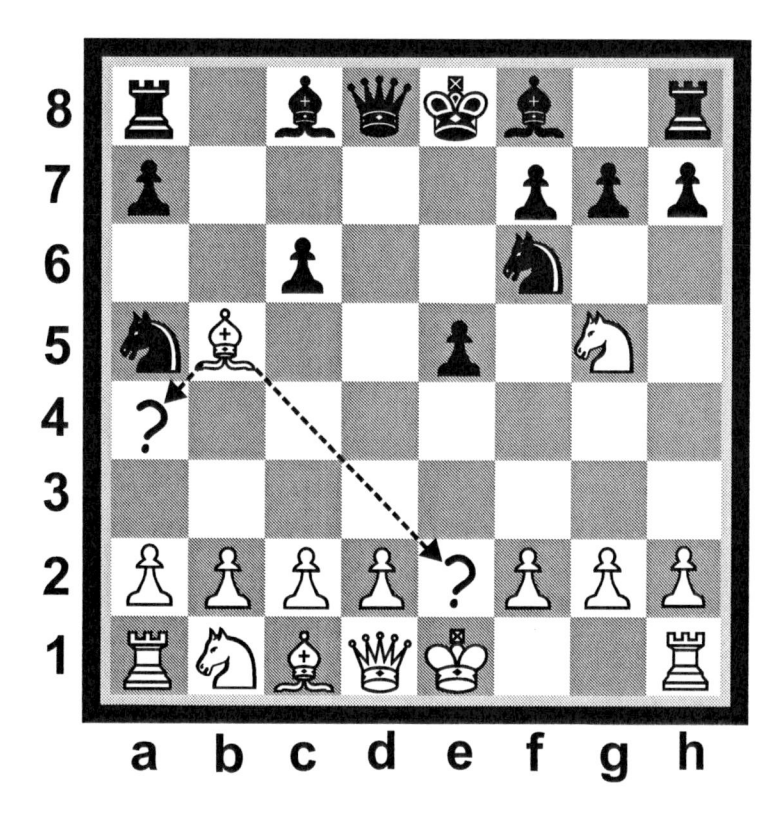

On Move 8, why is it better for White to retreat the Bishop to e2, rather than move to a4 and maintain the *pin* on the Pawn at c6?

Answer to
Activity 22, Two Knights Defense
Puzzle 4

White's move to a4 opens the possibility for Black to *fork* the Bishop at a4 and the Knight that will move to e5 (move 10). Follow the moves to see the *fork*.

8.	Ba4?	h6
9.	Nf3	e4
10.	Ne5	Qd4

The Black Queen *forks* the Knight and Bishop.

Note: The beginning player may believe that White can escape this *fork* and capture 1 of Black's Pawns. However, if White makes these moves, the White Knight will be trapped. Follow the moves to see the *trap*:

11.		Bxc6+ NxB
12.		NxN Qc5

The Black Queen at c5 has trapped the White Knight. At this position, Black has the advantage. This is another good point to practice playing with a clock.

Activity 23
Two Knights Defense
Puzzles 5 & 6

Puzzle 5

1.	e4	e5
2.	Nf3	Nc6
3.	Bc4	Nf6
4.	Ng5	d5
5.	ed (PxP)	Na5
6.	Bb5+	c6
7.	dc (PxP)	bc (PxP)
8.	Qf3?!	Rb8
9.	Nh3	_____

If, on move 9, White moves the Knight to h3 rather than to f3, should the Black Bishop at c8 take the Knight? Explain.

_____

_____

Puzzle 6

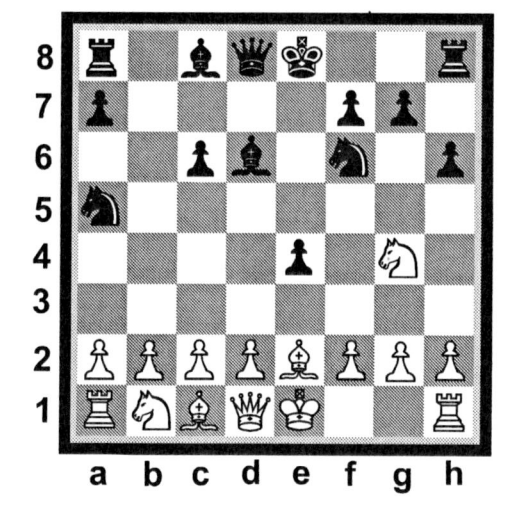

10.	QxN+	Nd7
11.	Ng4	

White has made move 11, Ng4, where it is attacked twice and defended twice.

Is this a good move for White? _____ Explain. _____

_____

Answer to Activity 23, Two Knights Defense Puzzles 5 & 6

Puzzle 5

No, Look at the game. Black should continue development, bringing the Bishop or Queen out. You do not have to take the White Knight immediately. Black only captures the Knight if White castles Kingside. The Knight is trapped; it has no moves except to retreat. In this setup, White should try to castle Queenside.

If White castles Queenside and Black castles Kingside, capturing the Knight is a mistake. When the Pawn captures the Bishop, White has an open g-file for the Rook to attack the Black King.

Note: White's pieces are not developed; Black's pieces are.

Puzzle 6

No, Black gets the advantage by bringing out the Queen. Follow these moves on your board.

| 11. Ng4 | Nxg4 |
| 12. Bxg4 | Qg5! |

There are several possible moves here for White.

| 13. Bxc8 | Qxg2 |
| 14. Rf1 | Rxc8 |

Here, White no longer has a Pawn advantage. Also, White still has no development and can't castle Kingside.

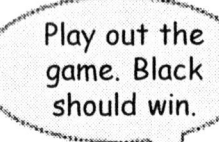

Play out the game. Black should win.

Chapter 7
Introducing the Fork Trick

The **Fork Trick** is an advanced pattern. But, if played correctly, it gives the player an advantage and, possibly, an easy win. Black can play the Fork Trick in a Two-Knights game against a player who really does not understand openings. The same pattern can appear in other openings. Follow the moves:

1. e4	e5
2. Nf3	Nc6
3. Bc4	Nf6

Black's third move attacks the unprotected Pawn at e4.

4. Nc3?!

Often, instead of responding with an aggressive move, such as Ng5 or castling, White moves the Knight to c3, protecting the Pawn. This allows Black to take the initiative with the Fork Trick.

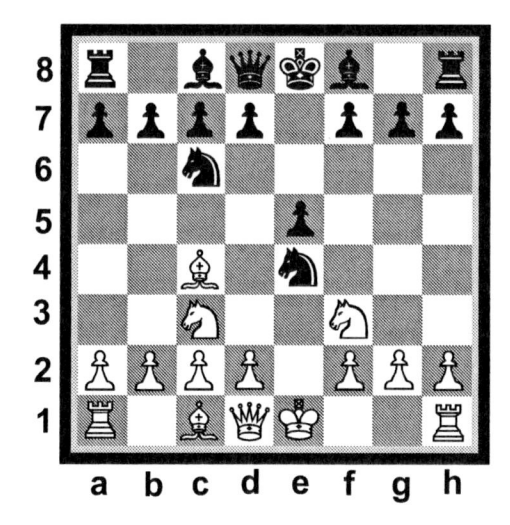

4. ...	Nxe4

This is the start of the Fork Trick. White has 2 possible moves. Many players consider the move Bxf7+ as giving White the advantage. Not so. (See *Activity: 26, Try to Stop the Fork Trick*, page 91)

The other possible move, NxN, is more common for White and leads to several variations of the Fork Trick. Let's follow this more common move.

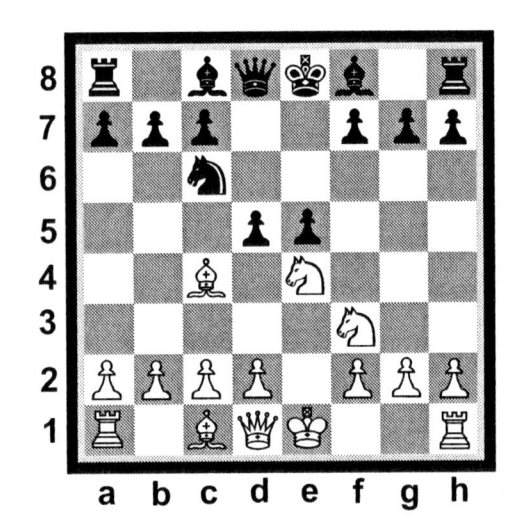

5. NxN   d5

With the move d5, the Black Pawn at d5 *forks* the Bishop at c4 and the Knight at e4. Black will win one of those pieces, not only making the game equal based on *material*, but also allowing Black to take the initiative and attack.

White has several choices, but none can save the piece:
1. Move the Bishop
2. Move the Knight
3. Move something else

Let's follow a common variation where White saves the Bishop and tries to create a counterattack, which will fail.

6. Bb5   dxN

White's move *pins* the Knight to the King at c6.

Black's move captures the Knight at e4 and attacks White's other Knight, forcing the Knight at f3 to move.

7. Nxe5   Qg5

The Knight that was threatened at f3 takes Black's Pawn at e5. Now, both White's Knight and Bishop are attacking Black's *pinned* Knight, which is protected only by a Pawn.

Black's Queen comes out, creating a tremendous attack on White's Pawn at g7, the Knight at e5 and, through it, the Bishop at b5. None of these are protected.

Look at the material. Right now, it's even. Let's follow Black's attack on the next page.

8. BxN+   **bxB**

BxN+ removes the threat of losing the Bishop at b5 to Black's Queen. Instead of losing the Bishop to the Queen, White makes an even trade — a Bishop for a Knight. White also maintains control of the move since Black has to get out of check, giving White the opportunity to save the Knight at e5 on the next move.

Note: This is the most common line of this variation. On move 8, White could move NxN or d4.

9. Nxc6   **Qxg2**

The White Knight has moved to safety and captured the Pawn at c6.

The Black Queen takes the Pawn at g2, threatens to take a Rook and prevents White from castling.

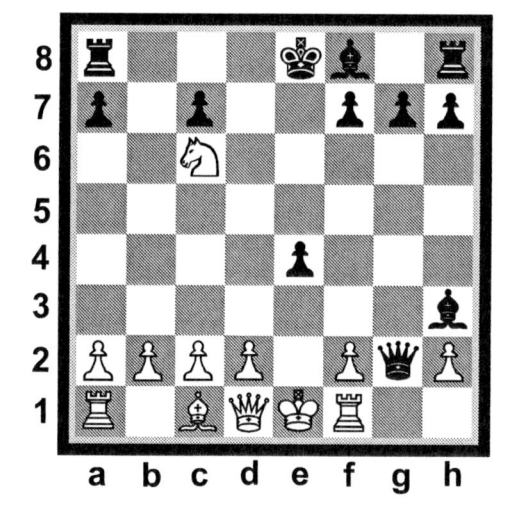

10. Rf1   **Bh3**

White's Rook moves to safety and Black brings the Bishop into the attack, threatening QxR checkmate.

11. Qe2

This move protects the Rook and stops checkmate.

11. ... QxR+

Black will trade the Queen and Bishop for the White Queen and Rook, a winning advantage.

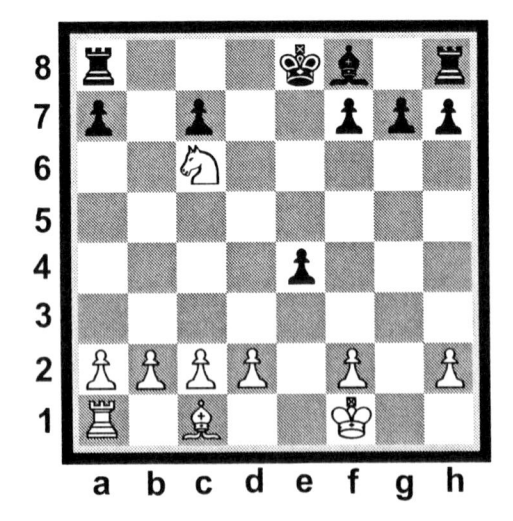

12. QxQ BxQ
13. KxB

Look at the material left at this point.

Of course, both sides have a King. Each side has 6 Pawns.

White has 1 Rook and 2 minor pieces for 11 points. The value of Black's pieces, 2 Rooks and a Bishop, is 13 points. This is a winning material advantage for Black.

The next steps in Black's plan:
1. Develop the Bishop (**Bd6**), attacking White's undefended Pawn at h2.
2. Develop the Rook at h8, either by castling or by moving the King to d7, attacking White's Knight.

This is one of the variations of the Fork Trick for Black. You'll be able to use it well if you practice.

Activity 24
Variations from Move 6 of the Fork Trick — Bd3

Once the Fork Trick occurs, White may choose to save the Bishop. In the main line, White saved the Bishop by moving Bb5. In this variation, White saves the Bishop by moving Bd3.

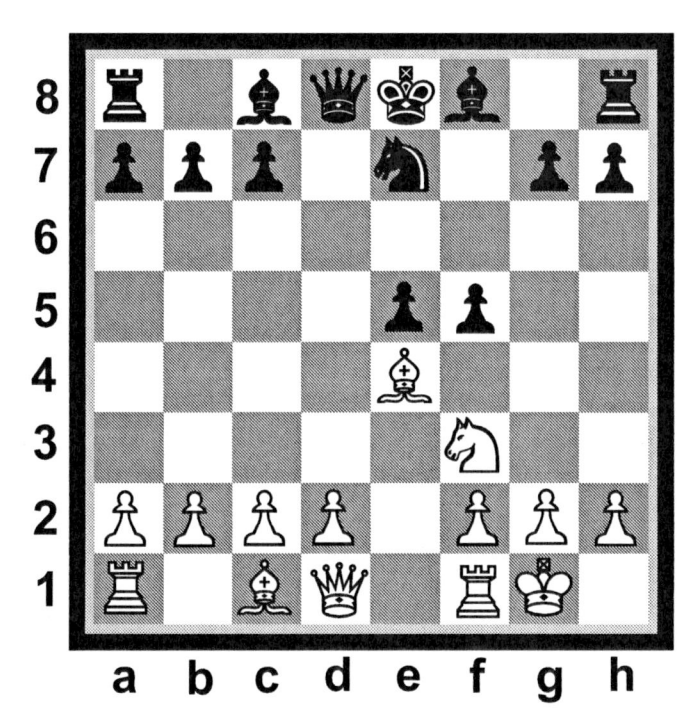

Play these moves, through move 8, on your chessboard.

1. e4	e5
2. Nf3	Nc6
3. Bc4	Nf6
4. Nc3	Nxe4
5. NxN	d5

With d5, Black forks the Bishop at c4 and the Knight at e4.

6. Bd3

White chooses to save the Bishop from the fork.

6. ...	dxN
7. Bxe4	Ne7
8. 0-0	f5

In this line, White loses a piece.

If White does not castle on Move 8, here are 3 other candidate moves.

1. What is Black's response to each?

    a. 8. Nxe5 _____

    b. 8. Bd3 _____

    c. 8. c3 _____

2. Who has the advantage after each move?

    a. _____

    b. _____

    c. _____

Answers to Activity 24, Variations from Move 6 of the Fork Trick — Bd3

1. Blacks response:

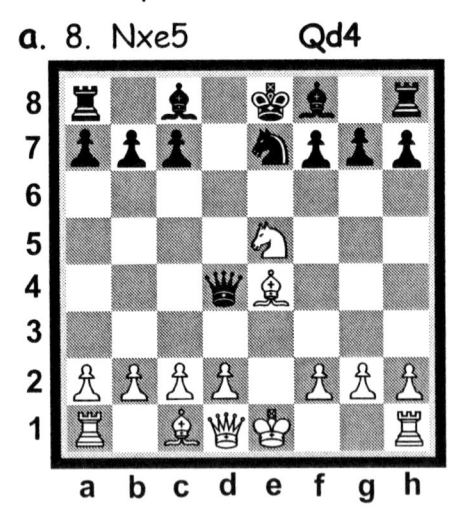

   a. 8. Nxe5   Qd4

   Black's move Qd4 forks White's Knight and Bishop.

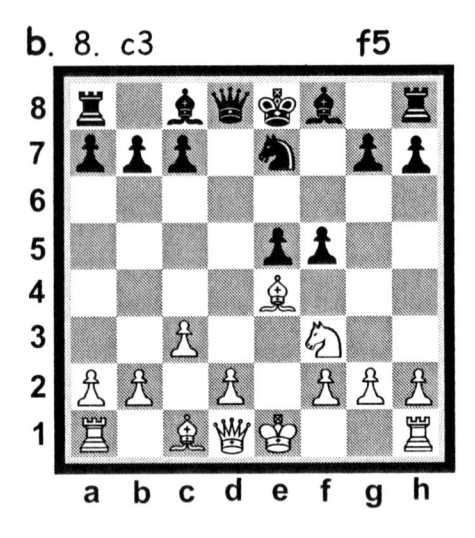

   b. 8. c3   f5

   Next, Move 9 for White should be Bc2 and Black responds with Nc6. This gives Black a strong center.

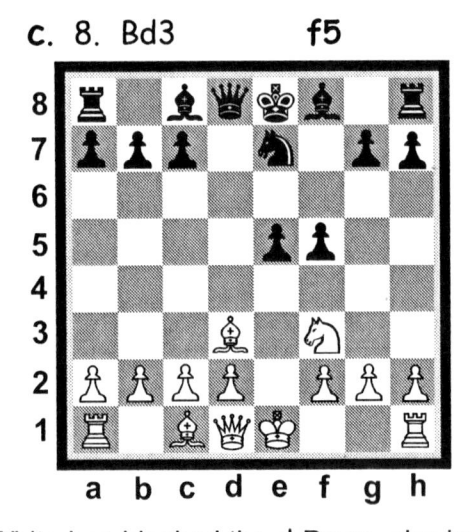

   c. 8. Bd3   f5

   White has blocked the d-Pawn, slowing down development.

2. Black has the advantage no matter which move White makes.

Activity 25: Extension
Variations from Move 6 of the Fork Trick — Bxd5

In this variation, White acts more aggressively by taking the *forking* Pawn. Play this variation on your chessboard.

1. e4	e5
2. Nf3	Nc6
3. Bc4	Nf6
4. Nc3	Nxe4
5. NxN	d5

With d5, Black forks the Bishop at c4 and the Knight at e4.

6. Bxd5

White takes the *forking* Pawn.

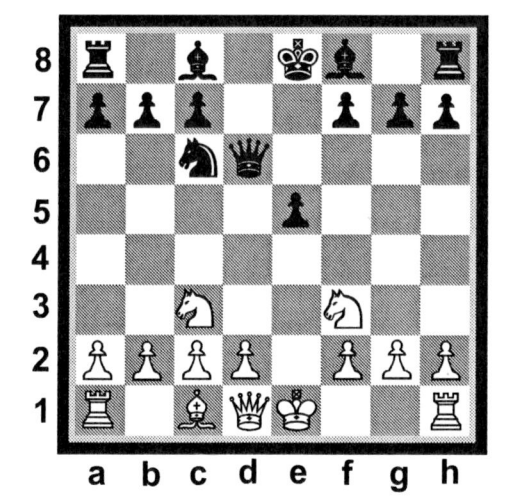

6. ...	QxB
7. Nc3	Qd6

To continue Black's plan, Black moves Bg4 and castles Queenside.

From this position play out the game.

You have now seen 3 lines from Move 6, for White, of the fork trick — Bb5, Bd3 and Bxd5. These ilustrate the best and most common moves for White after the Fork Trick.

Activity 26
Try to Stop the Fork Trick

1. e4   e5
2. Nf3   Nc6
3. Bc4   Nf6
4. Nc3   Nxe4

Here's the starting position, let's look at the variation.

The *fork trick* is a trade of a minor piece and a Pawn for a minor piece and a Pawn, where Black gains the initiative. In this variation, White attempts to keep the advantage.

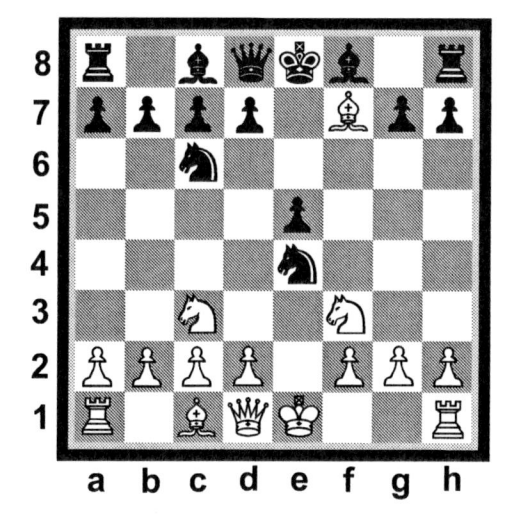

5. Bxf7+

With this move, White exposes Black's King, keeps Black from castling and prevents the *fork trick*.

5. ...   KxB

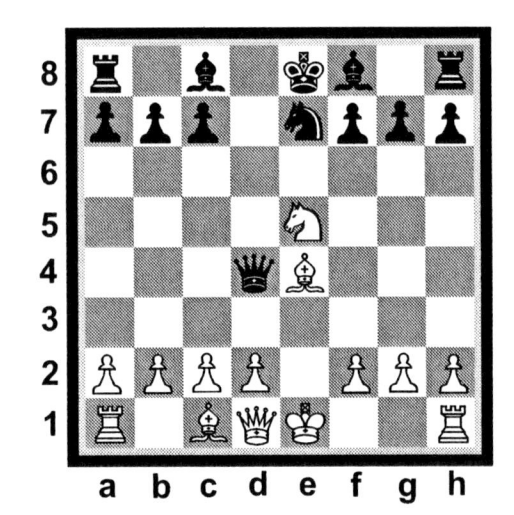

Black's King is forced to take the Bishop.

6. NxN   d5

White's Knight takes the Black Knight, leaving each side with 7 Pawns and 3 minor pieces.

Black's move to d5 is an attempt to take the initiative with an attack on White's Knight and the threat to control the center. This forces White's Knight to move.

7. Neg5+   Kg8

Kg8 seems safer than Ke8, but then it takes an extra move to get out the King Rook. This is a good position to try out both moves for the Black King. Black is better in both cases because it has control of the center.

8. d3   h6
9. Nh3   Bg4
10. Bd2   Bd6
11. Qe2   Kh7

Evaluate the position after move 11:

1. Compare the position for White and Black. _____

2. Compare the material for White and Black. _____

3. What move can further Black's plan? _____

Chapter 7
Fork Trick Activities

Answer to
Activity 26, Try to Stop the Fork Trick

1. Black has a space advantage and controls the center.
2. The material for both sides is even, but White's pieces are hemmed in.
3. Black needs to get the Rook into the game: **Rf8**

Note: When Black's King was forced to move before castling, Black was still able to set up a castling position, with the King safe and the Rook developed. Look at the King moves for "castling by hand." In this opening the King goes to h7 in 3 moves before the Rook moves to f8.

Castling by Hand #1

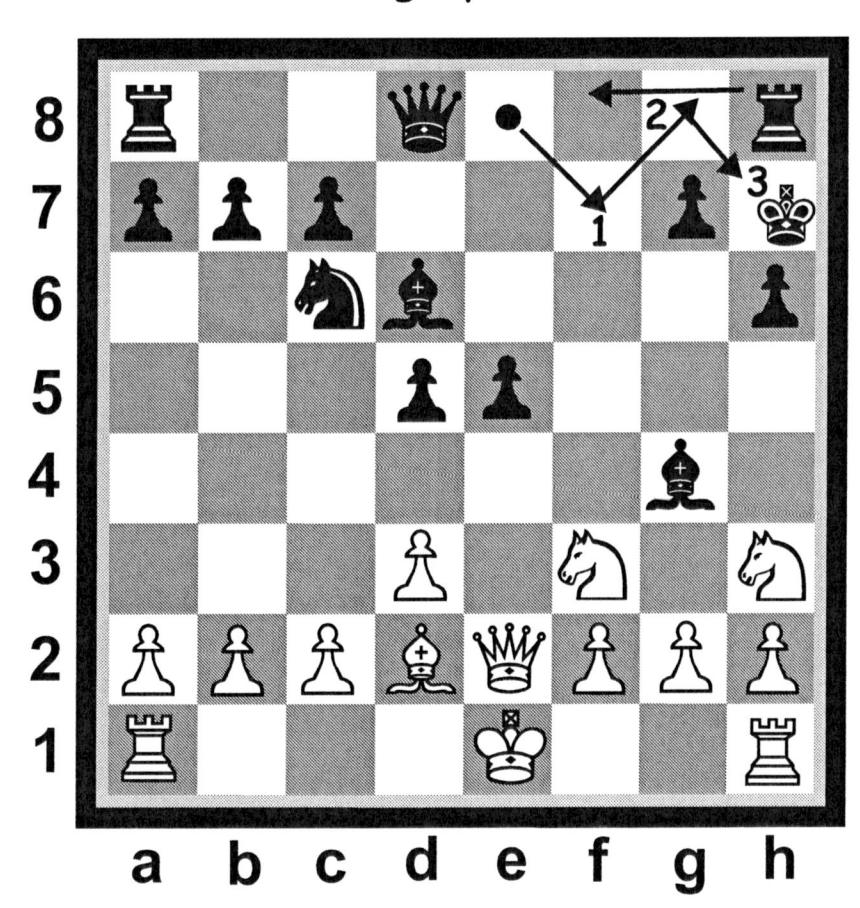

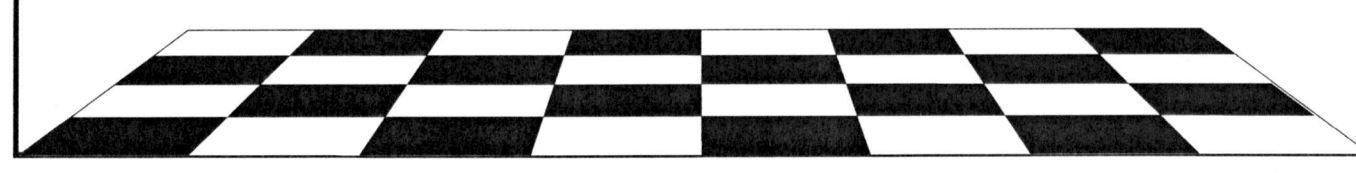

Chapter 8
The Fried Liver Attack

The **Fried Liver Attack** is a variation of the Two Knights Defense. It is called *Fegatello* in Italian.

This opening follows the same moves as the Two Knights Defense — up to the point of White's 5th move. Look at the position at this point.

1. e4　　　　　　　　　e5
2. Nf3　　　　　　　　Nc6
3. Bc4　　　　　　　　Nf6
4. Ng5　　　　　　　　d5
5. ed (PxP)

White has captured a center Pawn. It would be natural for Black to try to maintain equality by capturing a center Pawn.

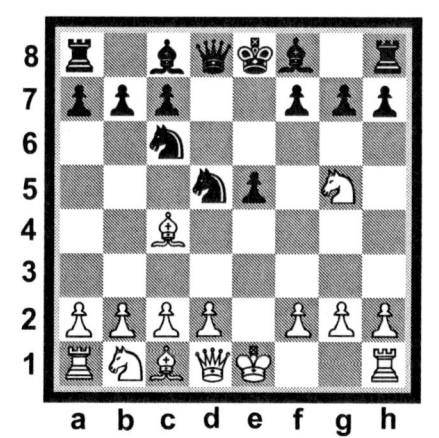

5. ...　　　　　　　　　Nxd5

Nxd5 looks like the natural move. After the capture of the Pawn, it looks like Black has the advantage in the opening. Black has well-developed pieces and the Queen is attacking White's unprotected Knight at g5.

But, White is ready to castle and Black's Knight at d5 is *pinned*. If it moves, White will have 2 pieces attacking f7, which is defended only by the King.

6. d4

This move allows White's Knight at g5 to be protected by the Bishop. But, White's Pawn at d4 is protected only by the Queen and it is attacked by both Black's Knight and Pawn. It seems as though White has made a blunder and will lose the d-Pawn.

Note: The way the Fried Liver Attack was originally played, at move 6, White's Knight would immediately capture the Pawn at f7. (See Activity 27, page 99.)

Actually, White's move 6 is a trap to encourage Black to take the Pawn, either by moving Nxd4 or ed. If Nxd4, see Activity 28, page 101, for the possible moves.

6. ... ed
7. O-O

White continues development, waiting for Black to develop the Bishop at f8.

7. ... Be7

Note: This is Black's most common move for the Bishop.

8. Nxf7!?

Finally, Black has moved the Bishop from f8, getting ready to castle. This signals White to start the *Fried Liver Attack*, Nxf7.

With this move, White forks Black's Queen and Rook. This move also stops Black from castling and it forces the Black King to move to the center of the board (6th rank).

8. ... KxN
9. Qf3+

Black's King is forced to take White's Knight or lose either the Queen or the Rook.

White brings the Queen into the attack, checking Black's King and, simultaneously, attacking the Knight at d5. Now both White's Queen and Bishop are attacking this Knight, which is protected only by the Queen.

9. ...   Ke6

Black's King gets out of check and adds additional protection to the Knight at d5. The Knight is still *pinned*.

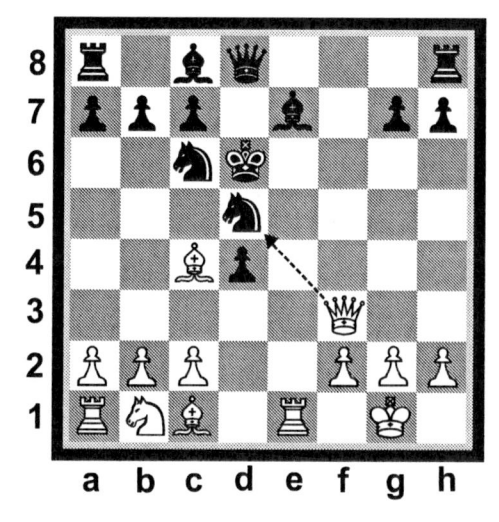

10. Re1+   Kd6???

White gets the Rook into the attack.

Black's move out of check is a terrible blunder. On the next move, White's Queen takes the Knight at d5 and checkmates the King.

Black's better 10th move would have been Kd7 to avoid checkmate. However, White would still have the advantage.

The Fried Liver Attack is one that White is able to play often in this opening. Whether it's played immediately, or in a delayed version, it is aggressive, fun and should win for White.

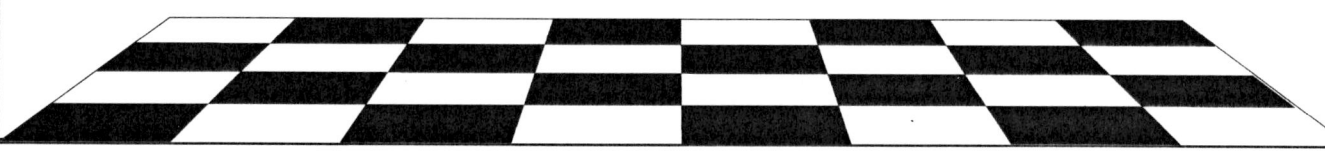

Activity 27
White Wins a Knight

In this activity, instead of 6. ... ed, Black takes the Pawn with the Knight.

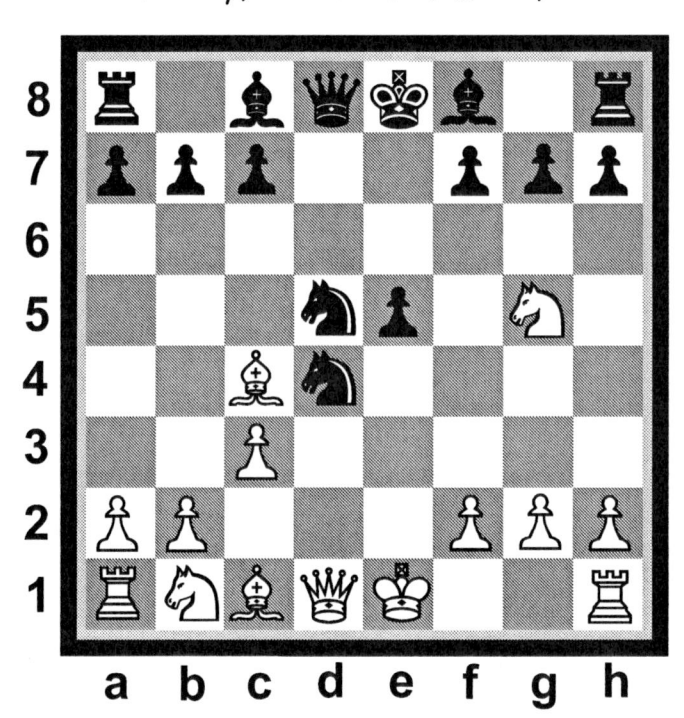

6. ... Nxd4?
7. c3

With c3, White chases the Knight away.

Play through the rest of the moves of this puzzle on your chessboard.

1. If the Knight goes back to c6, the Black Knight at d5, which was attacked only by the Bishop, will now also be attacked by the Queen. White wins the Knight.

2. If the Knight goes to e6, White must then play QxN, winning the Knight at d5, which threatens checkmate.

7. c3	Ne6
8. QxN!	QxQ
9. BxQ	NxN
10. BxN	

Play out both of these possible variations to make sure you understand them.

White wins the Knight.

Activity 28
The Original Fried Liver, Forks and Pins

Originally, the Fried Liver Attack was played this way: at move 6, White's Knight would immediately capture the Pawn at f7.

1. e4   e5
2. Nf3   Nc6
3. Bc4   Nf6
4. Ng5   d5
5. ed (PxP)   Nxd5 (NxP)

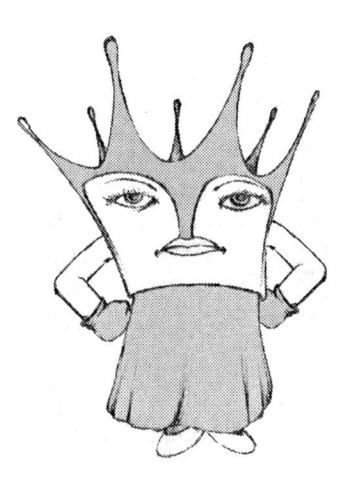

Position 1

6. Nxf7!?

Nxf7 *forks* Black's Queen and Rook and forces Black's King to take the Knight, rather than lose either the Queen or the Rook. Normally, it's not a good move to sacrifice a piece for a Pawn just to prevent the King from castling. But, it forces the Black King to move to the center of the board (6th rank). and draw him off the back rank.

This is an exception. Why? _____

_____

Position 2

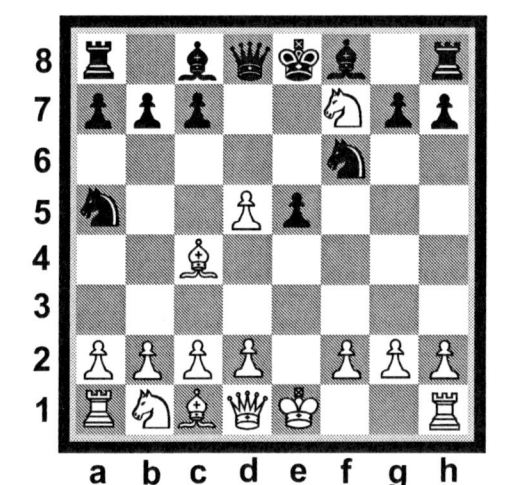

In a similar position:

5. ...   Na5
6. Nxf7?

Once again, Nxf7 *forks* Black's Queen and Rook and forces Black's King to take the Knight, rather than lose either the Queen or the Rook. However, the results for White will be dramatically different. Why?

_____

_____

_____

_____

Answer to Activity 28
The Original Fried Liver, Forks and Pins

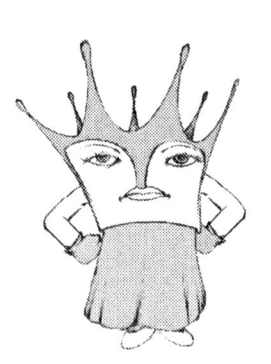

Position 1: Strong for White

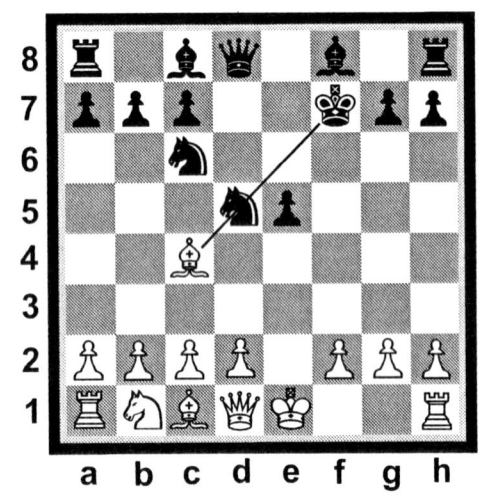

Black's capture here increases the power of White's *pin* on the Knight at d5 because now it is pinned to the King at f7, an *absolute pin*.

Note: Whenever you have a piece pinned, you will want to attack it as many times as possible to gain the advantage. On the next move, White can attack the pinned Knight by moving either Qf3+ or Nc3.

Position 2: Weak for White

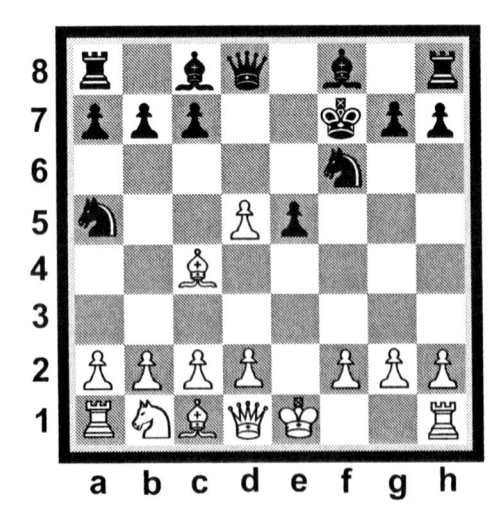

1. KxN gives Black a free Knight.
2. There is no *pin* for White.
3. Black's Knight at a5 currently threatens White's Bishop at c4.
4. The White Queen cannot safely attack the King.

Activity 29
The Fried Liver Attack, Puzzles 1 & 2

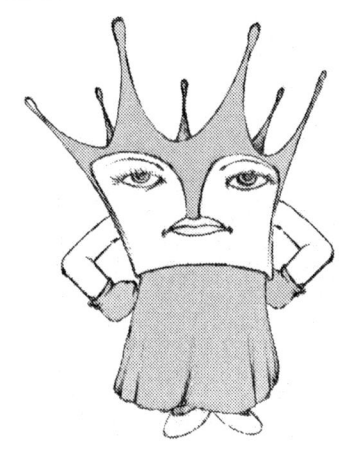

1. e4   e5
2. Nf3   Nc6
3. Bc4   Nf6
4. Ng5   d5
5. ed   NxP (Nxd5)
6. Nxf7   KxN

Puzzle 1

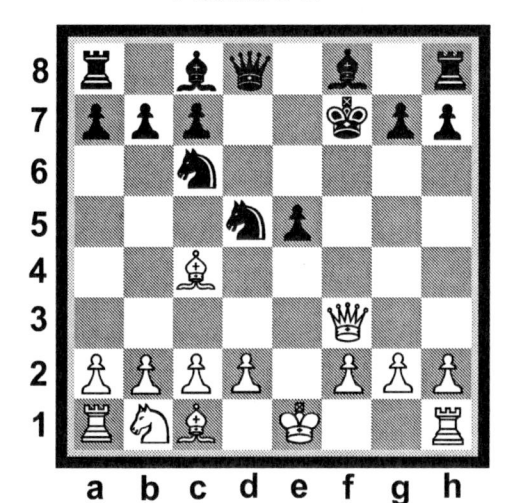

7. Qf3+

Here, White's Queen attacks the pinned Knight and checks the King. The Black Knight is now attacked twice and defended only once by the Black Queen.

What are Black's best moves? _____

_____

_____

Puzzle 2

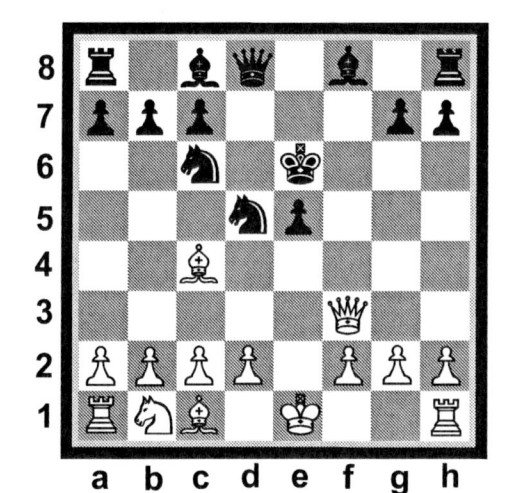

7. ...   Ke6

At this point, White has given up the Knight for a Pawn and forced the Black King toward the center of the board.

What are *candidate moves* here for White?

_____

_____

_____

_____

Answers to
Activity 29
The Fried Liver Attack, Puzzles 1 & 2

Puzzle 1

7. ... Ke6

This is the only move for Black.

The King must **move** to **e6** to maintain the advantage, get out of check **and** protect the Knight a second time.

Note: The Knight is still pinned by the Bishop.

Puzzle 2

1. Nc3, attacking the pinned Knight once again.
2. Qe4, pinning Black's Pawn at e5, with the plan to attack that pinned Pawn once again.
3. Castle.

Play games from this position, trying each of White's candidate moves.

Activity 30
The Fried Liver, Puzzles 3 & 4

Puzzle 3

8. Nc3

With this move, Black's pinned Knight is attacked 3 times and protected only twice.

What should Black do? _____

_____

Puzzle 4

In this position:

a. What are the *candidate moves* for Black?

b. How does White respond?

_____

_____

Answers to Activity 30
The Fried Liver, Puzzles 3 & 4

Puzzle 3

To protect the Knight at d5 a third time, Black must move the Knight at c6 to e7 or b4.

Puzzle 4

Possible Answer 1

a. 10. ...   Ne5
Black blocks the check.
b. 11. Qe4

Possible Answer 2

a. 10. ...   Kd7
King escapes to a safe square.
b. 11. BxN

Note: White has the advantage in both cases.

Chapter 9
The Power of the Pin

The *pin* is the easiest of all chess tactics and it is easy to set. It's an attack against 2 or more of an opponent's pieces in a straight line — diagonal, rank or file.

For example:

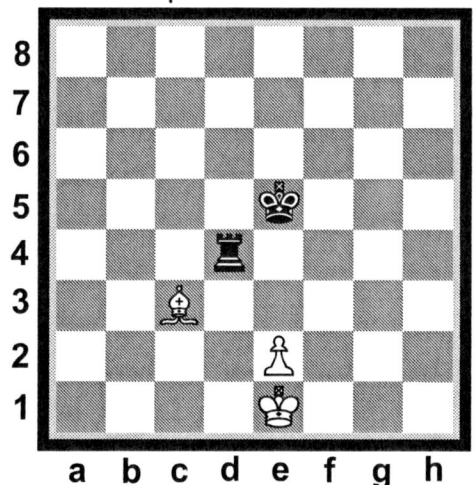

The White Bishop is *pinning* the Black Rook to its King. The Rook cannot move.

The Bishop is the *pinning piece.*

The Rook is the *pinned piece.*

The King is the *shielded* (protected) *piece.*

Note: This is an *absolute pin*. The shielded piece is a King and it is illegal to move the Rook, the pinned piece, and put the King in check. The Rook could move if the *shielded piece* was the Queen; but, a piece — the Queen — could be lost.

Let's look more closely at this position. If the White Bishop takes the Black Rook, the King takes the Bishop. This looks like a good trade for White because a Rook is more valuable than a Bishop. Actually, this trade will lead to a draw only. Try it.

Piling On

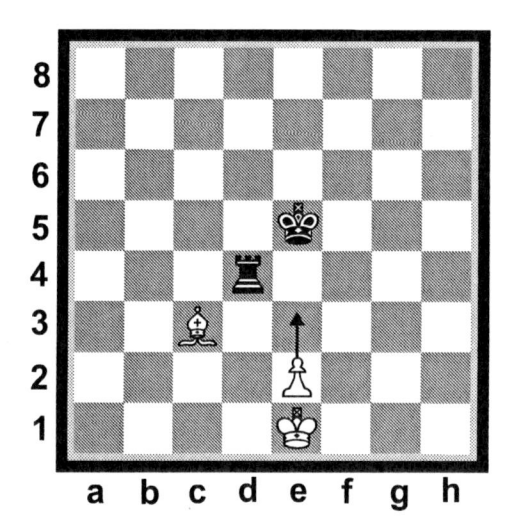

There's a better way to take advantage of a pin. When you set a pin, immediately begin to apply more pressure to the pinned piece by attacking it with other pieces. Example: From our position, it is a better move for White to move the Pawn to e3, attacking the Rook a second time, rather than take the Rook. This is called "piling on."

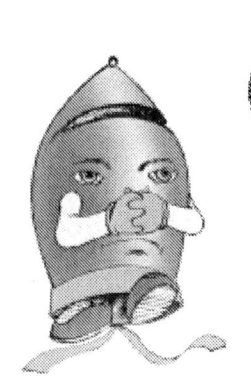

From this point, White can win rather than draw.

Activity 31
The Power of the Pin, Puzzles 1 & 2

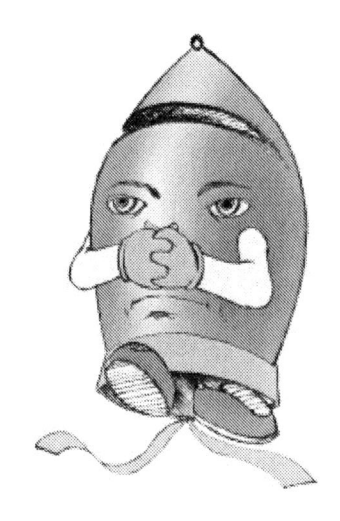

Puzzle 1

White to move:

1. How can White *pin* the Rook?
   _____

2. How does White *pile on* the attack?
   _____

3. How many moves until White wins the Black Rook?
   _____

Puzzle 2

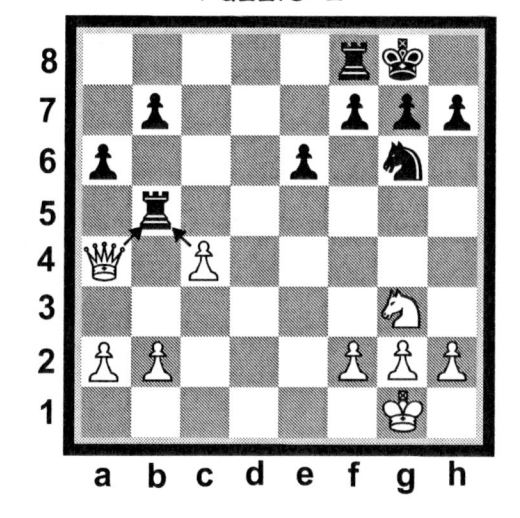

White to move:

1. What is *pinned* and how?
   _____

2. What can White do to take advantage of the *pin*?
   _____

Answers to
Activity 31 The Power of the Pin, Puzzles 1 & 2

Puzzle 1

1. Qa4 (the *pin*)   **a6**

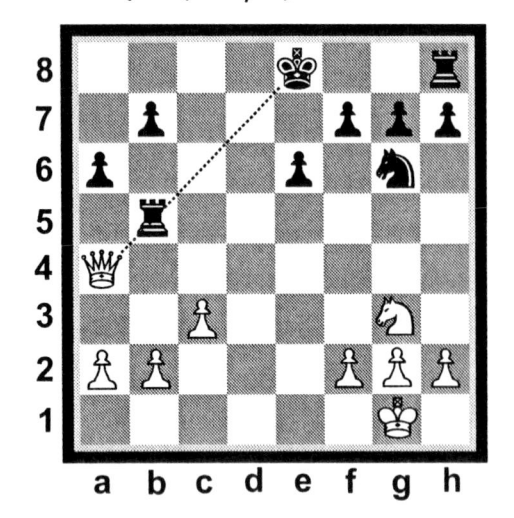

2. c4 (*piling on*)   **0-0**

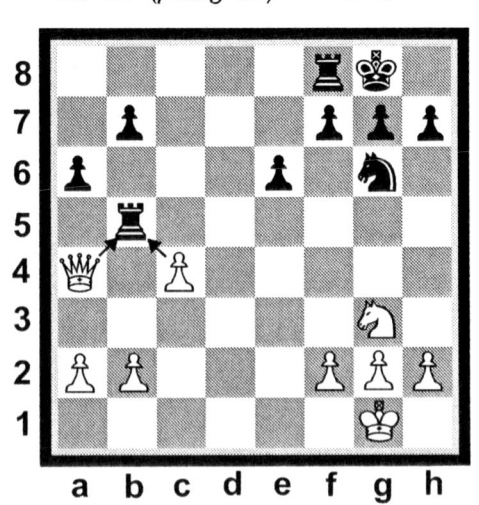

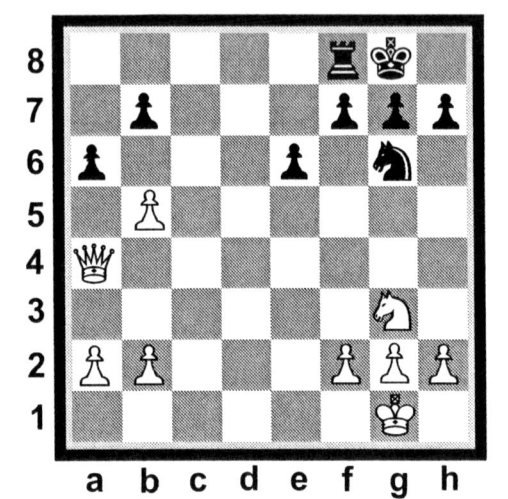

3. cxR (PxR)

Note: If Black were unable to protect the Rook with the Pawn move to a6, the Queen would have immediately won a free Rook. Once Black castles, the Rook is not pinned, but it's already lost.

Puzzle 2

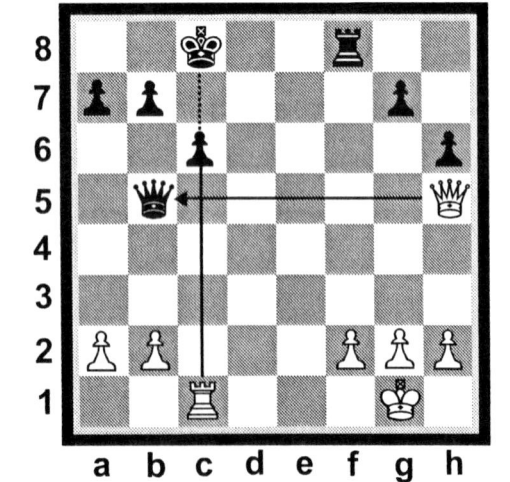

1. The Black Pawn at c6 is *pinned* to the King by the White Rook at c1.

2. White's best move is QxQ because the Pawn cannot capture. White gains a free Queen because of the *pin*.

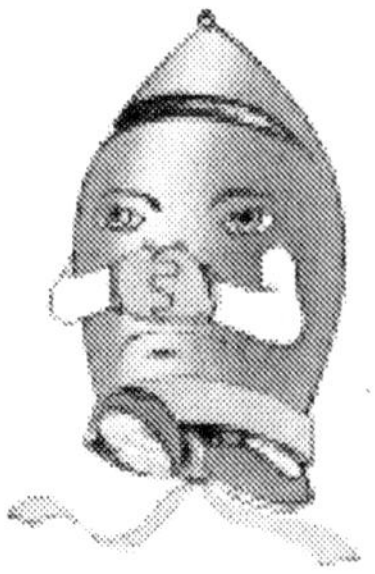

Copyright © 2002, 2005 Teachable Tech, Inc.
All Rights Reserved.

Chapter 9
Power of the Pin Activities

Activity 32
The Power of the Pin, Puzzle 3

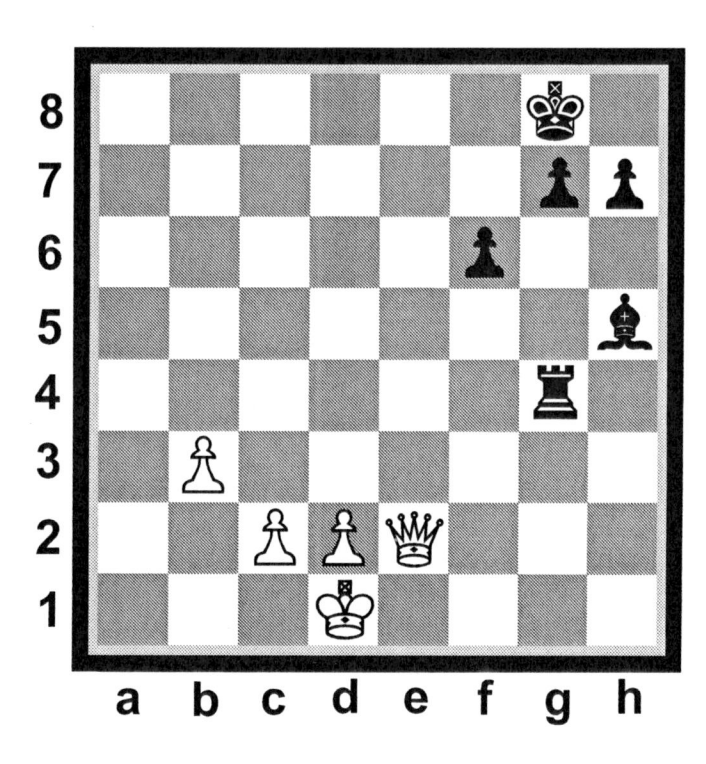

Black to move:

1. How does Black set the pin to win the Queen? _____

    _____

2. How does Black set the pin to get checkmate? _____

    _____

Answers to Activity 32
The Power of the Pin, Puzzle 3

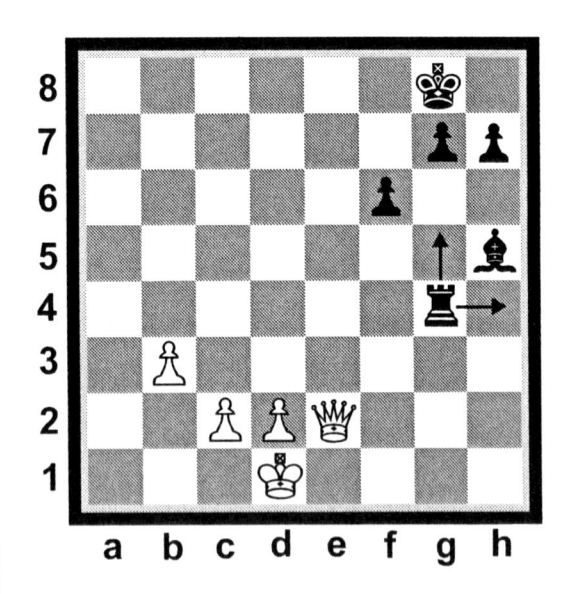

The Queen is *pinned* to the King — as soon as the Black Rook moves, the Bishop is attacking the Queen that cannot move to safety.

There are 2 possible ways for Black to set the *pin*.

1. The Rook could move to either g5 or h4 to protect the Bishop, allowing the Bishop to safely attack the Queen.

— OR —

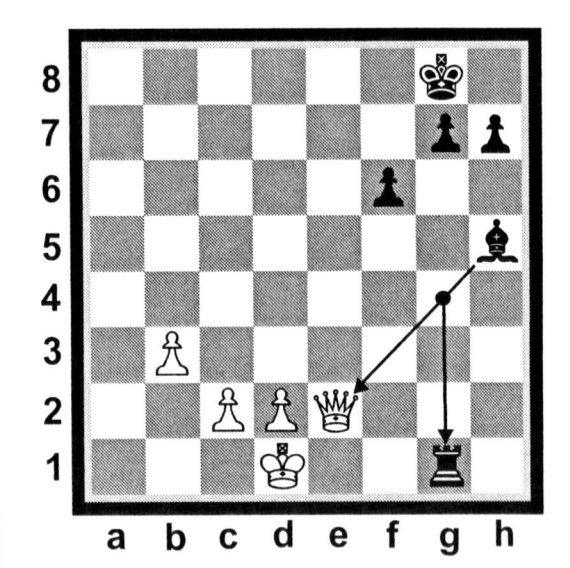

2. The Rook could move to g1, checking the King, while the Bishop still attacks the Queen pinned to the King. Since the Queen cannot move to block the check by the Rook, and the King is trapped on the back rank, it's checkmate.

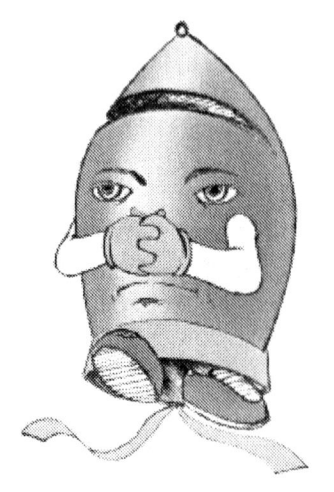

Chapter 10
The Stonewall Attack

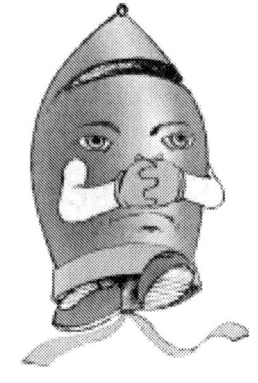

The **Stonewall Attack** is a Queen-Pawn Opening, beginning with the first move, d4. The opening move to d4 is the second most powerful opening. However, it is much safer than e4.

The **Stonewall Attack** is a sharp, open attack. But, with a Queen-Pawn style opening, Black is expecting a closed, positional game. Black then follows a standard Queen-Pawn opening pattern.

Note: Many scholastic players will make *copycat* moves because they are not used to a Queen-Pawn opening.

The game that follows is an actual game played between a coach vs. a scholastic player.

1. d4	d5
2. e3	e6

Black's first 2 moves are examples of *copycat* moves.

Note: Black can stop the Stonewall if, on move 2, Black moves Bf5, rather than *copycat* with e6.

3. Bd3

Bishop to d3 is key to this opening — it is the start of the **Stonewall Attack**. This Bishop (the Stonewall Bishop) must be protected and kept active; its value is more than the 3 points a Bishop is usually assigned.

3. ...   Nf6

This is a typical opening move for Black.

DANGER! White must try to prevent Black from blocking the Stonewall Bishop on the b1 to h7 diagonal.

4. Nd2   c5

White's move prevents the Black Knight from moving to e4. White is attacking e4 with both the Knight at d2 and the Bishop at d3.

DANGER! Black's move threatens to force the Stonewall Bishop off the b1 to h7 diagonal if, on its next move (move 5), Black's Pawn moves to c4.

Note: Nc6 is a *variation* on the 4th move for Black. This move also threatens to attack White's Stonewall Bishop by moving Nb4 on the next move (move 5).

5. c3   Be7

With the possibility of a threat on the Stonewall Bishop, White had to move c3 to give the Bishop a means of escape to c2. White continues to maintain control of the b1-h7 diagonal. Black continues development.

6. f4

With the White pawns building a stone wall on the dark squares, White will use the pieces to build a second stone wall attacking the white squares.

Note: At this point, Black has developed more pieces and appears to have a better position. White has a good start on building the stone wall that will block in Black and prevent many good moves.

6. ...   0-0
7. Ngf3   Nc6

Kingside castling with the Knight on the f-file is a strong defensive position for Black. Now, Black only has to get the Queen and the Bishop off the back rank to complete development.

Note: It seems that Black is slightly more developed because White will have difficulty developing the Queen-Bishop. However, in the Stonewall, the Queen-Bishop is usually blocked in for a while.

8. O-O   Bd7
9. Ne5

With Ne5, the Knight becomes an *outpost* and White has completed a double stone wall. The wall is built with White's Pawns on black, attacking black squares, and White's pieces attacking light squares. White has control of the majority of the board and prevents Black from mounting an effective attack.

Note: Many players will say White has too many light square weaknesses. But, Black can't mount an attack, and White attacks using the light squares.

9. ...   Qc7

Black gets the final piece off the back rank so the Rooks are connected. But, the Stonewall has cramped Black's position; Black has few good moves.

10. g4

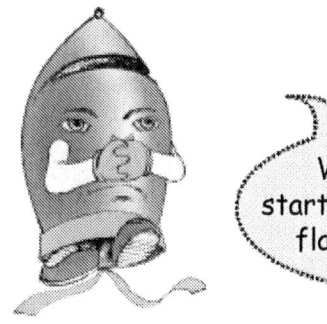

White has started a Kingside flank attack.

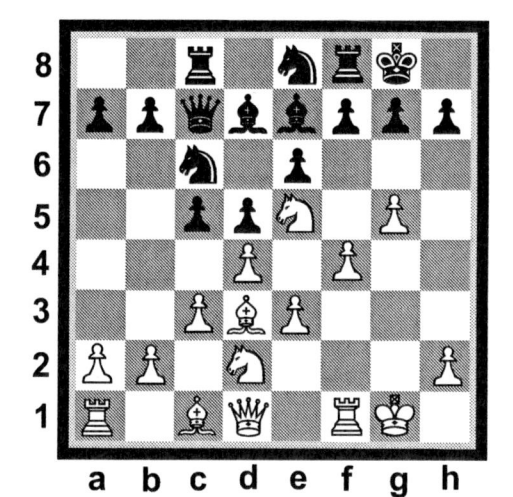

10. ...   Rac8

Note: Either Rook could have moved to c8 at this time. Notation describes which Rook moves.

11. g5   Ne8

With White's move to g5, the Pawn attacks the Knight at f6. Black's Knight must escape to e8. White has chased away a defender of the castled King.

Chapter 10
The Stonewall Attack

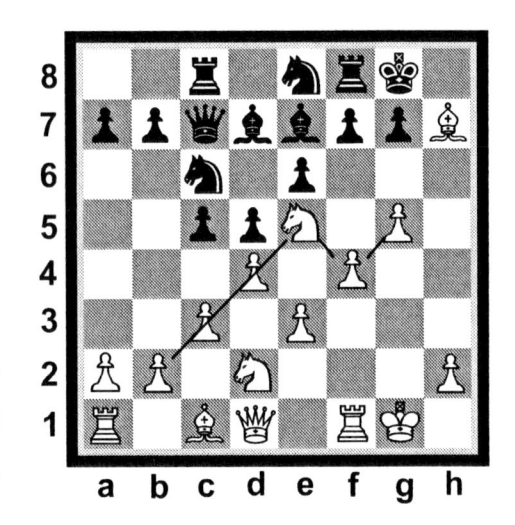

12. Bxh7!+

The wall is complete; the attack begins.

Note: White must be sure of the plan for a winning position before sacrificing the Bishop at h7. From this position, the Bishop sacrifice leads to a win.

From a slightly different position, White may have to improve the development of his pieces before starting the attack. For example, if Black's Bishop is at d6, instead of e7, White must lift the Rook to f3 before the Bxh7 sacrifice.

These first 12 opening moves are from a fairly typical game. Black's moves may vary during the opening. But, with thought, White can continue building the stone wall and carry out the planned attack. If at any point Black foils White's plan, just continue play, while looking for development and attack.

White has the advantage from this position. Study the following 12-move winning combination.

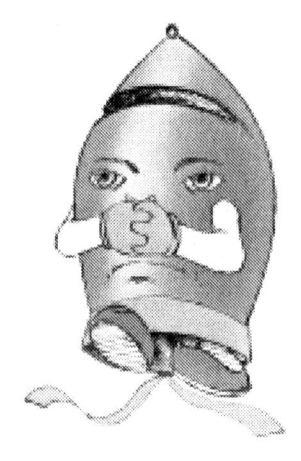

12. ...   KxB

White has sacrificed the Bishop to expose the King to attack.

Chapter 10
The Stonewall Attack

13. Qh5+	Kg8
14. Rf3	g6
15. Qh6	Ng7
16. Rh3	

White's Queen and Rook form a *battery*. A *battery* adds power.

16. ...	Nh5

Black's best plan: Get the Knight back into the game. The move to h5 separates White's Queen-Rook *battery*.

17. Nxg6

In this move White sacrifices his Knight to further open Kingside. White removes the *guard* of the Black Knight at h5.

17. ...	f7xN
18. Qxg6+	Ng7

Once again, White removes the guard to the Knight, checking the King. The Knight is no longer safe and moves back to g7 to block the Queen check.

19. Rh8!+

From the position at the start of the attack, Move 12, White had a forced win. Starting with this Rook sacrifice, White has a forced checkmate in 4 moves.

Note: White has already sacrificed a Bishop and a Knight to gain 3 Pawns. Now, on Move 19, White sacrifices the Rook for a brilliant win. There is also a win for White, Move 19, Rh7.

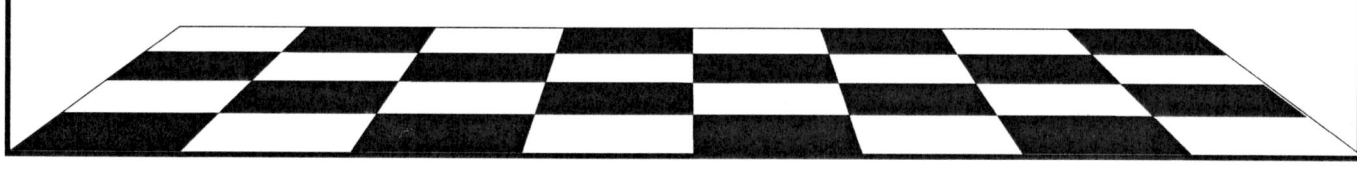

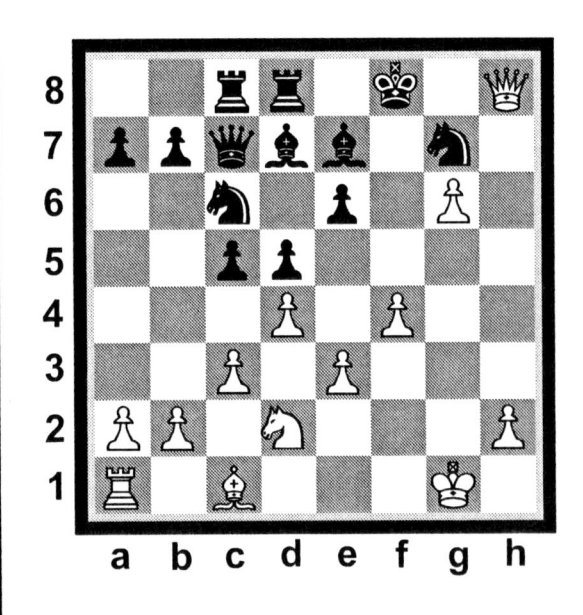

19. ...	Kxh8
20. Qh6+	Kg8
21. g6	Rfd8
22. Qh7+	Kf8
23. Qh8#	

The Stonewall pattern can be used in many openings for White. Black can also use this opening against a Queen-Pawn opening. Then, it's called the *Dutch Defense*.

See Activity 38 on page 129 for the notation for the Stonewall Attack for Black, usually called the Dutch Defense.

Activity 33
The Power of the Stonewall Attack

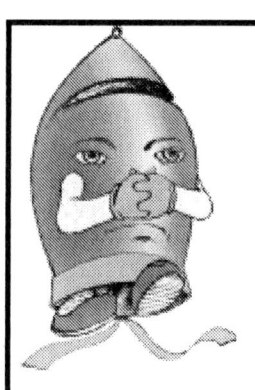

Even in the opening for a *closed game*, you can create a tremendous attack using the patterns that you learn from the Stonewall — with the proper planning. Follow this general plan:

1. Keep open the diagonals for the Queen and the Bishop.
2. Have a plan to "lift" the Rook easily into the attack.
3. Have a Knight as an outpost, also attacking the castled King.

Without this system, beginning players will have difficulty mounting this attack in a closed game.

In the sample game, page 113-118, the stone wall is built after the 11th move for White. Show the power of this position:

1. Place an X in every light square attacked by a White piece.
2. Place a O in every dark square attacked by a White Pawn.

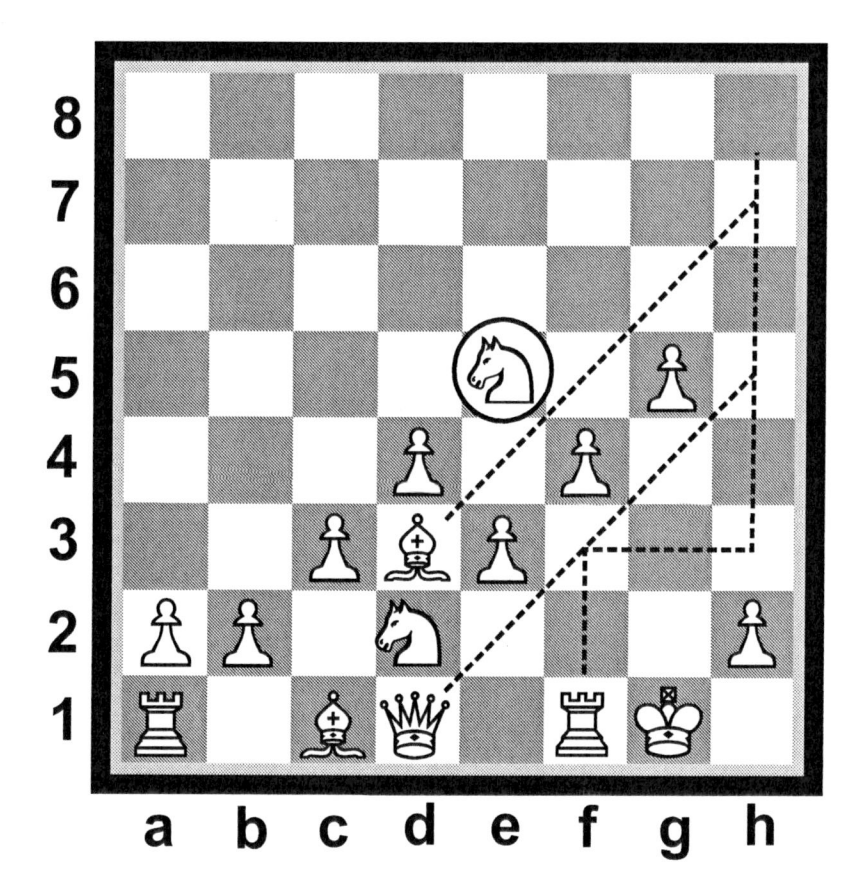

Chapter 10
The Stonewall Attack Activities

Answer to
Activity 33
The Power of the Stonewall Attack

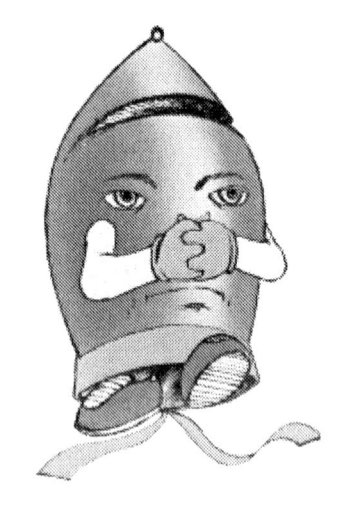

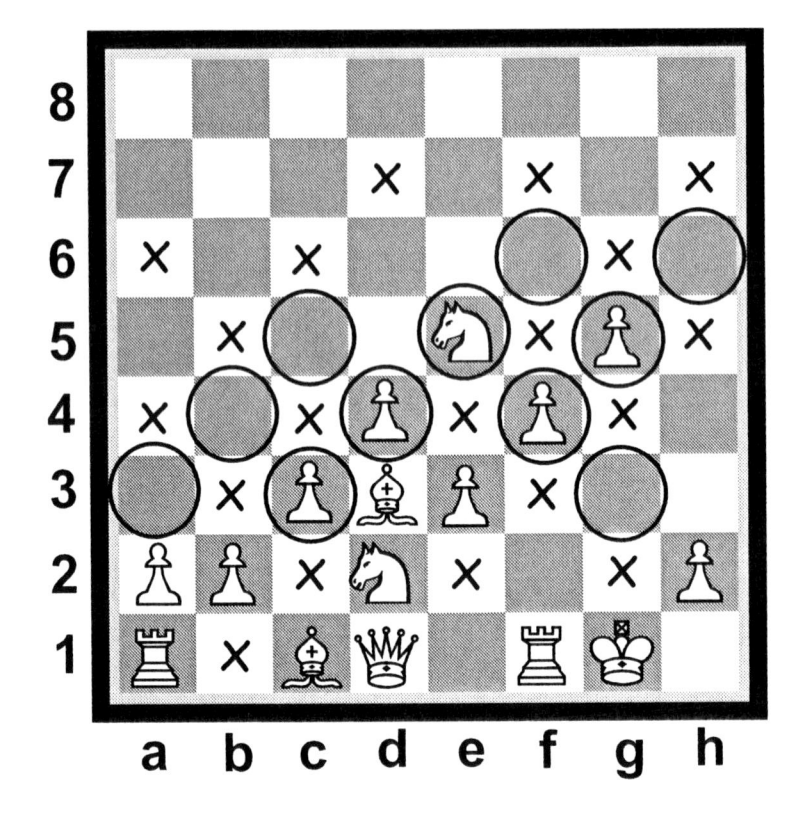

Chapter 10
The Stonewall Attack Activities

Activity 34
Building the Wall

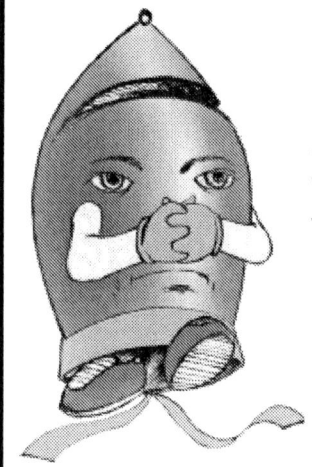

On the score sheet below, show the first 11 moves that would build a wall for White. The order of White's moves may differ according to Black's moves. But, the stone wall we have studied should still be built.

White's Moves for the Stonewall Attack

EVENT					Date
Round	Board	Section	Time Control	Opening	
				Stonewall Attack	
WHITE					
BLACK					

#	White	Black	#	White	Black
1			7		
2			8		
3			9		
4			10		
5			11		
6			12		

Chapter 10
The Stonewall Attack Activities

Answer to Activity 34
Building the Wall

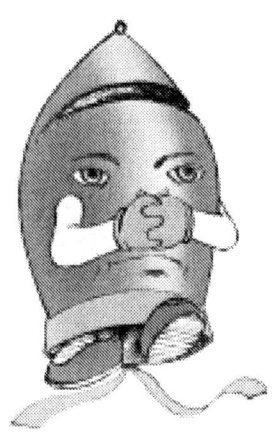

White's Moves for the Stonewall Attack

EVENT					Date
Round	Board	Section	Time Control	Opening	
				Stonewall Attack	

WHITE

BLACK

#	White	Black	#	White	Black
1	d4		7	Ngf3	
2	e3		8	0-0	
3	Bd3		9	Ne5	
4	Nd2		10	g4	
5	c3		11	g5	
6	f4		12		

Look at the diagram on the bottom of page 119 to see the Stonewall position.

Note: This is an opening for White, so we're not showing the best moves for both White and Black. Since there are very few trades in closed games, either this position, or one very similar to it, occurs often.

Activity 35
The Stonewall Attack
Puzzles 1 & 2

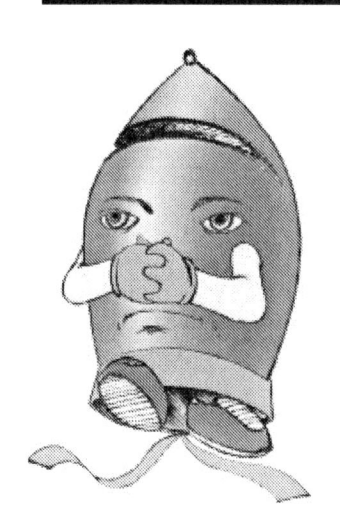

Puzzle 1

White's first 2 moves signal a possible Stonewall Attack.

1. d4   d5
2. e3

What is the simplest way for Black to stop a possible Stonewall Attack?

_____

_____

Puzzle 2

2. ...   Nc6

On move 2, Black moves Nc6 rather than Nf6.

♟ What are Black's threats?

_____

_____

♟ What is White's best move?

_____

_____

Copyright © 2002, 2005 Teachable Tech, Inc.
All Rights Reserved.

Chapter 10
The Stonewall Attack Activities

Answers to Activity 35
The Stonewall Attack, Puzzles 1 & 2

Puzzle 1

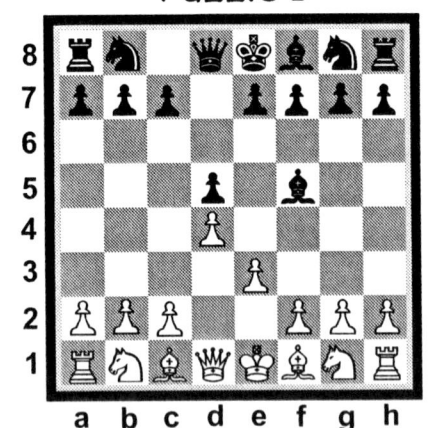

The simplest way to stop the Stonewall Attack on move 2 is for Black to take control of the Stonewall diagonal by moving Bf5.

Note: Black has prevented the White Bishop from taking control of the diagonal. But, White still has the tactic to try to gain a Pawn by challenging Black on the diagonal, moving the Bishop to d3.

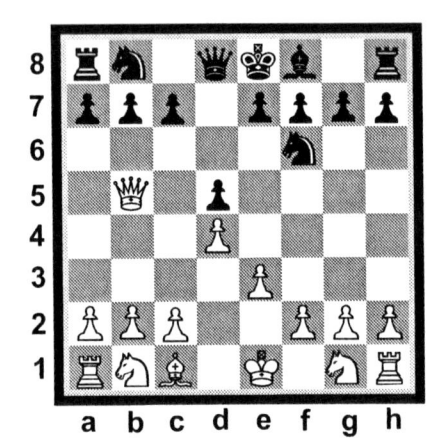

3. Bd3	Bxd3
4. Qxd3	Nf6?
5. Qb5+	

Nf6 is normally a good developing move. In this case, it allows White to create a double attack, checking the King and attacking the unprotected Pawn at b7. Black cannot protect both, so it loses the Pawn.

To prevent this problem, Black should, on his 4th move:

4. ...	c6

Puzzle 2

♟ Black has 2 threats: Nb4 to threaten the Stonewall Bishop on the Knight's next move; and, Pawn to e5, which threatens to block the Stonewall Bishop on the Pawn's next move to e4.

♟ White's best move is f4. This prevents Black's threat of e5, but must delay White's developing the Stonewall Bishop to d3.

Note: Often, you will have time to set up a Stonewall pattern because it's a slower moving, closed game. Your opponent, unfamiliar with your opening, will be playing a slower, closed game giving you time to set your pieces.

Activity 36
The Stonewall Attack
Puzzles 3 & 4

Puzzle 3

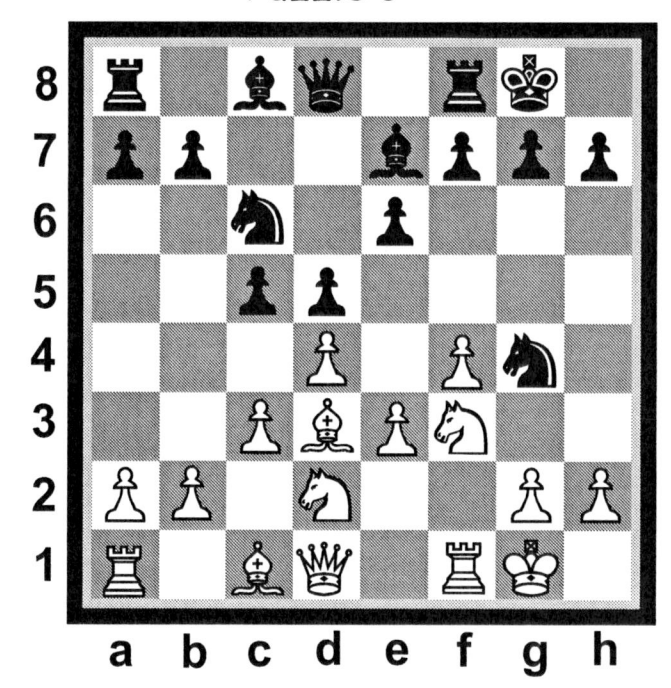

What's White's best move from this position — Black's Knight at g4 attacks the unprotected Pawn at e3?

_____

Puzzle 4

In many cases, the Black Bishop is often at d6. If the Black Knight then goes to g4, White has a dynamic attacking move. What is it?

_____

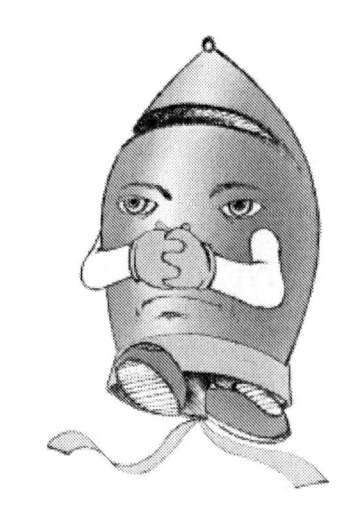

Answers to
Activity 36
The Stonewall Attack, Puzzles 3 & 4

Puzzle 3

White moves **Qe2**.

Or...

White moves **Ng5**.

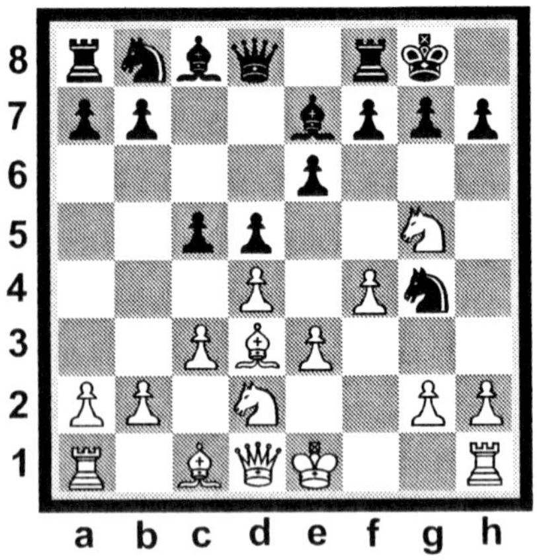

Note: There is often more than one "right" answer in chess.

Puzzle 4

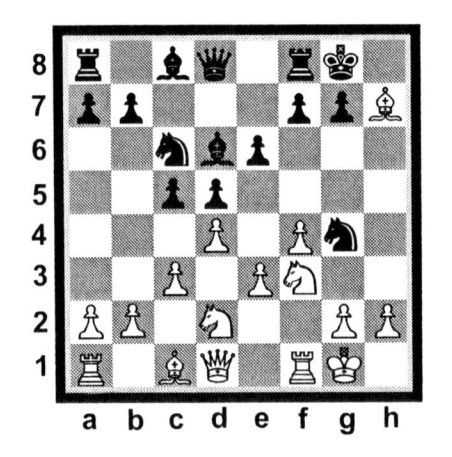

White's best move is **Bxh7+**.

Follow the moves to see what happens.

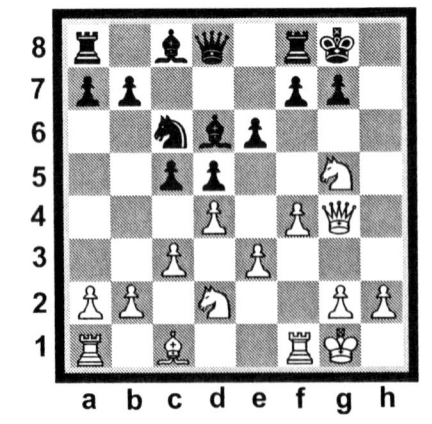

9.	Bxh7+	K×B
10.	Ng5+	Kg8
11.	Q×N	

Here, White has traded the Stonewall Bishop for a Knight and a Pawn. The Knight defender is removed, opening up Black's King.

Challenge: Play both White and Black from this position. See if you can win with White's advantage.

Activity 37
The Stonewall Attack
Puzzles 5 & 6

Puzzle 5

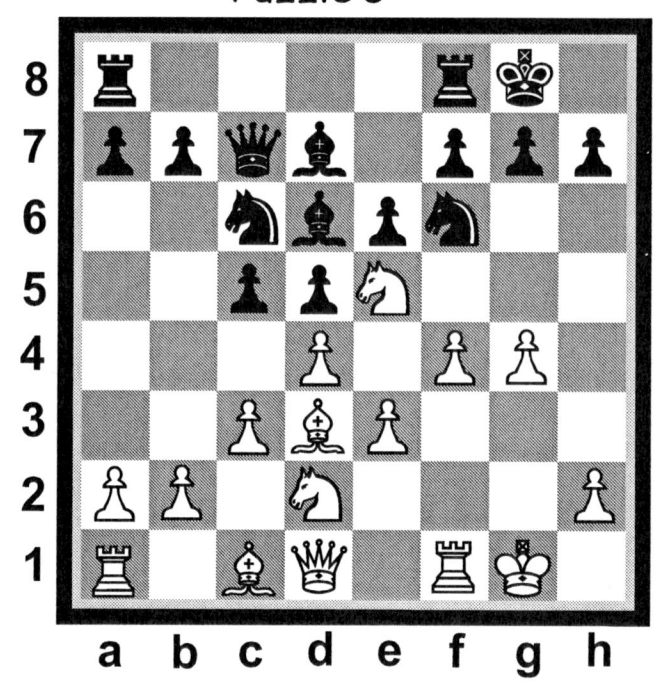

Look at the diagram. Notice the Bishop at d6. If Black takes White's outpost Knight, BxN, what is White's best move?

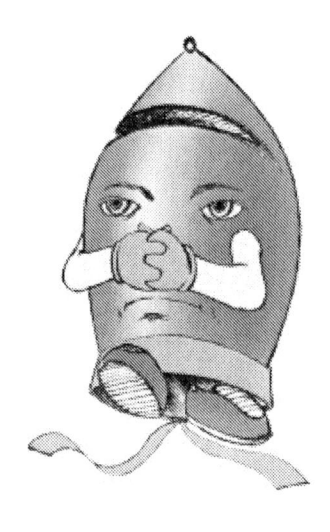

_____

Puzzle 6

Look at the diagram. Notice the Bishop is at e7 instead of d6, as in Puzzle 5. Black's Knight has taken White's *outpost* Knight at e5. What is White's best move?

_____

Remember: the plan is to be able to push the g-Pawn forward.

Answers to
Activity 37
The Stonewall Attack, Puzzles 5 & 6

Puzzle 5

fxB   P(f)xB

Chasing Black's Knight to e8, the only square it can move to safely.

Note: White's plan is to push the Pawn to g5.

Puzzle 6

dxN P(d)xN

Note: Puzzles 5 and 6 are very similar. White's *outpost* Knight is taken in both cases. The key difference is the location of Black's dark-square Bishop.

In the Stonewall, when White's outpost Knight is captured, White prefers to take the Black piece with the f-Pawn to make it easier for the Bishop at c1 to come into the game, as in Puzzle 5. But, when Black's Bishop is at e7, you must capture with the d-Pawn. If you moved the f-Pawn, your g-Pawn could not advance safely.

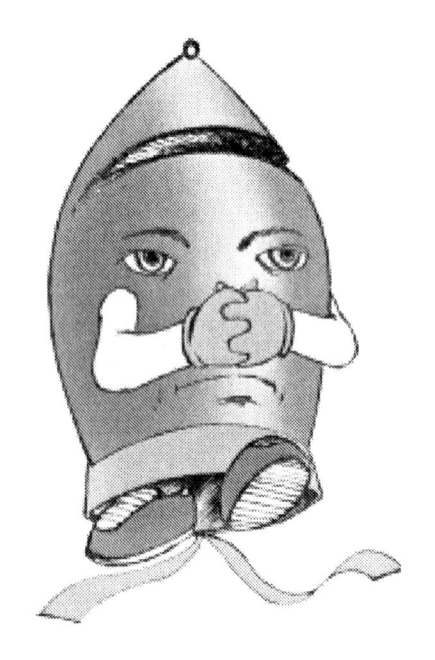

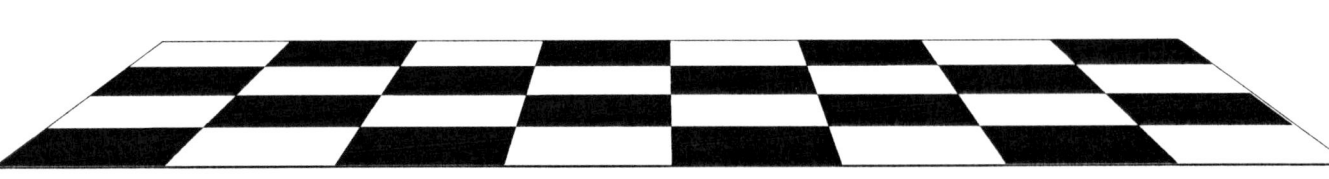

Activity 38

The Stonewall Attack for Black
(aka The *Dutch Defense*)

Originally called the *Dutch Defense*, the Stonewall was played for Black against Queen–Pawn openings. The patterns are the same as the Stonewall for White; only, the colors are reversed. The Black Pawns will attack light squares; the Black pieces will attack dark squares. Most beginners have difficulty playing against a Queen–Pawn opening, so the Dutch Defense is a good plan. And, you've already learned it as the Stonewall.

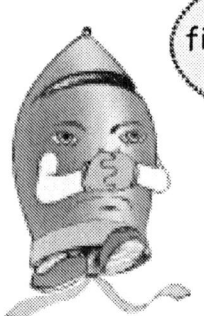

Here are the first 12 moves of the Dutch Defense.

1. d4   d5
2. c4   c6
3. Nc3   e6
4. e3   Bd6

The Stonewall Bishop for Black is at d6, controlling the b8-h2 diagonal. This Bishop always attacks the Kingside so that it can capture the Rook–Pawn and check the King.

5. Nf3   Nd7

DANGER! When White moves the Knight to f3, threatening to block the b8-h2 diagonal, Black moves the Knight to d7 to stop the threat.

6. Be2	f5
7. O-O	Ngf6
8. Bd2	O-O
9. Qc2	Ne4
10. c5	Bc7
11. b4	g5
12. b5	g4

At move 12, Black has completed the stone wall. The Stonewall Bishop in the Dutch Defense is poised to begin the attack on the next move.

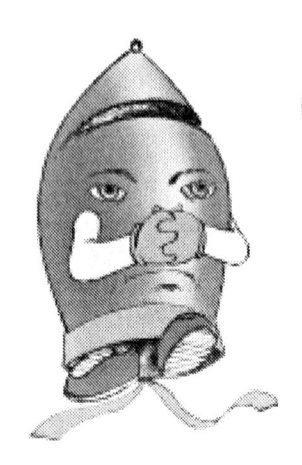

Follow these moves to complete the game.

EVENT

Round	Board	Section	Time Control	Opening

WHITE

BLACK

#	White	Black	#	White	Black
13	Ne1	Bxh2+	19	fxN	Qxg3+
14	KxB	Qh4+	20	Ng2	Rh1!+
15	Kg1	Rf6	21	KxR	Qh3+
16	g3	Qh3	22	Kg1	g3
17	Ng2	Rh6	23	Rfd1	Qh2+
18	Nh4	Nxg3	24	Kf1	Qh1#

In this variation of the Dutch Defense, the position differs slightly from the previous one. Note move 6: the White Bishop moves to d3 rather than e2. Black can continue the Stonewall pattern, but there is no longer the same forced win.

Move the Rook from f8 to f6 before the sacrifice, to add more power to the attack and ensure a winning position.

1. d4   d5
2. c4   c6
3. Nc3   e6
4. e3   Bd6
5. Nf3   Nd7
6. Bd3   ...

Remember, always study the position carefully.

Chapter 11
Taking Advantage in the Opening

It is important to memorize the openings, but it's more important to understand opening strategy. When your opponent makes a move in the opening that is not what you expect, stop and think: "Is it a blunder? Can I take advantage of it?"

Below is an ideal set up for opening development for White. In reality, the ideal rarely happens. But, if you take advantage of your opponent's blunders, you can take the advantage in the game.

#	WHITE	BLACK	#	WHITE	BLACK
1	e4		5	Bc4	
2	d4		6	Bf4	
3	Nf3		7	0-0	
4	Nc3		8		

White has accomplished the 3 principles of openings — control the center, develop pieces rapidly and castle early.

Look at the 2 examples on this and the next page.

Example 1

1. e4   b6
2. d4!

White controls the center with the first 2 moves — e4 and d4. No matter what opening plan you have if, on your second move you can safely put a second Pawn into the center, do it!

Example 2

1. e4	e5
2. Nf3	Nf6
3. Nxe5	Nxe4
4. Qe2	Nf6?

Black's first 3 moves are copycat moves. When White moves Qe2, the White Queen and Knight are lined up with the Black King. When Black moves the Knight from e4 back to f6, White can take advantage of the blunder.

With the Black Knight removed from the e-file, the only thing between White's Queen and Black's King is White's Knight.

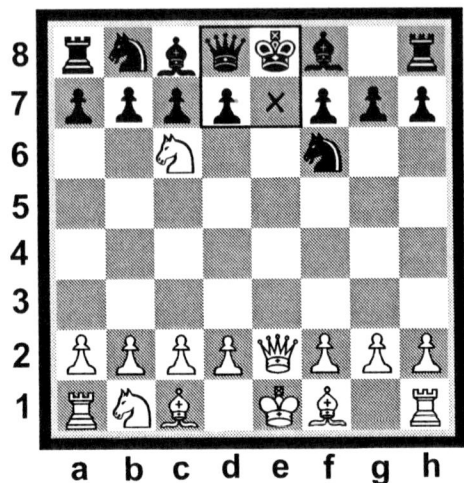

5. Nc6+ (discovered check)

It's White's move: Any move of White's Knight is discovered check. With the move to c6, the Knight attacks the Queen. The only square the Queen can move to is e7.

Note: Had the White Knight moved Ng6, White would have gained a free Rook.

Now practice taking advantage of the opening with the next 2 puzzles.

Chapter 11
Taking Advantage in the Opening

Activity 39
Taking Advantage in the Opening, Puzzle 1

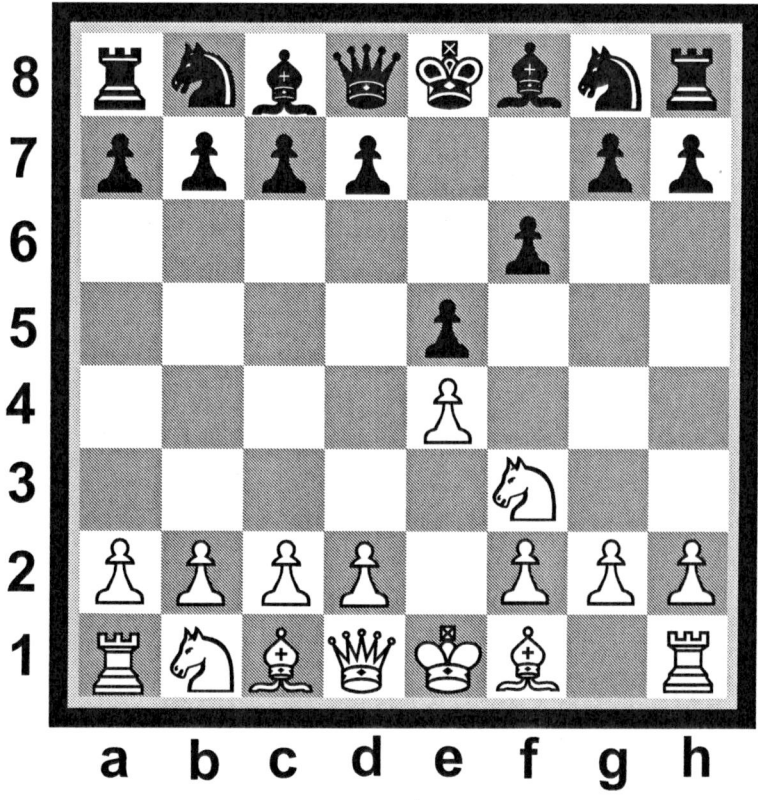

1. e4   e5
2. Nf3   f6

Black's second move protects the Pawn, but it's not the move you've learned. Is it a mistake? Can White take advantage of it?

Answer to Activity 39
Taking Advantage in the Opening, Puzzle 1

YES! It's a mistake. And, **YES!** White can take advantage of it.

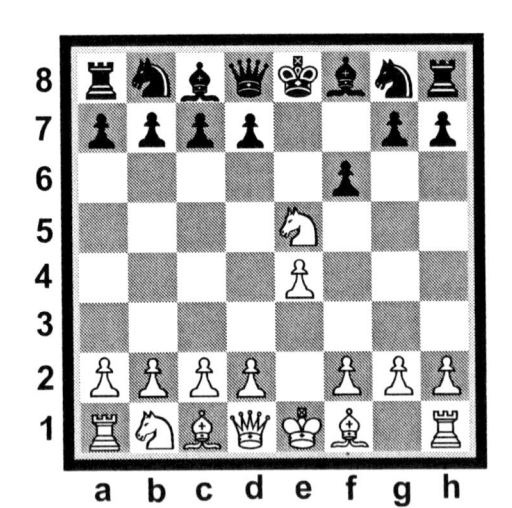

3. Nxe5

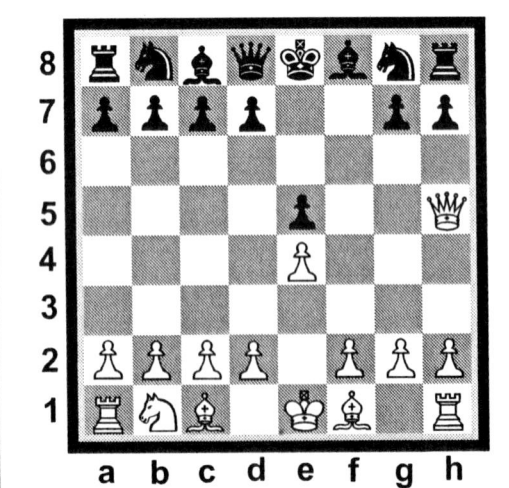

3. ...   f6xN

4. Qh5+

Note: With Queen to h5, White is now able to play the Queen's Raid. Without the Pawn at h7, it's an immediate check. Black has 2 choices — block the Queen with Pawn to g6 or move the King to e7. Either move loses. Play out both possibilities.

Copyright © 2002, 2005 Teachable Tech, Inc.
All Rights Reserved.

Chapter 11
Taking Advantage in the Opening Activities

Activity 40
Taking Advantage in the Opening, Puzzle 2

Here's an actual game played on the Internet.

1. e4   b6
2. d4   g5
3. Bxg5   f6
4. Qh5#

What are Black's blunders? _____

_____

What did White do to take advantage of these mistakes? _____

_____

Answers to Activity 40
Taking Advantage in the Opening, Puzzle 2

Black's Blunders:

Move 1: ... **b6**

    Failure to fight for control of the center

Move 2: ... **g5**

    Failure to fight for control of the center

    Failure to develop a piece

    Loss of a Pawn

Move 3: ... **f6**

    Opens lines to the King

    Failure to develop a piece

White's Advantage:

Moves 1 and 2: **e4, d4**

    Take control of the center

    Open lines for the Bishops

Move 3: **Bxg5**

    Develops a Bishop

    Captures a Pawn

Move 4: **Qh5#**

    Looks at attacking the King

Note: White's Bishop is under attack. The first instinct is to move to safety. But, by always checking for attacks on the King or Queen, White was able to see the checkmate.

The Basics: Moves and Captures

Let's review.

Pawn

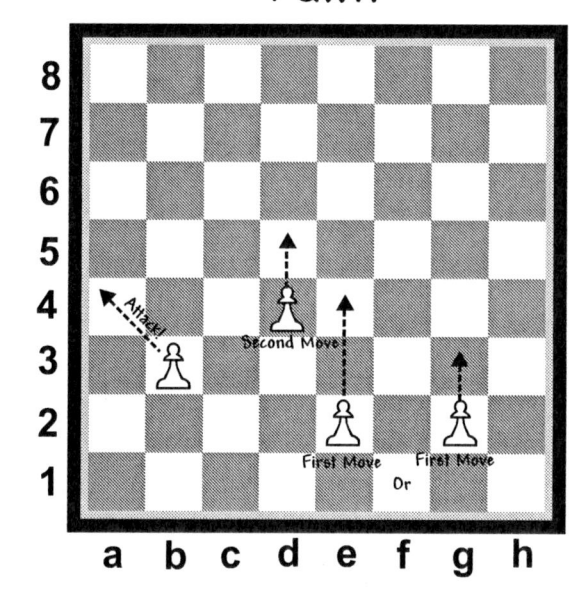

Pawns are out on the front lines when the game begins — White Pawns at Rank 2, Black Pawns at Rank 7.

A Pawn may only move forward. On its first move, and only on its first move, each Pawn may move 2 squares or 1 square. On all other moves, Pawns must move only 1 square.

Pawns are the only pieces that capture differently than they move. Pawns capture on the diagonal one square forward. Pawns are the only piece that can never move backward. Because they cannot "back up" and capture on the diagonal, Pawns can easily be blocked by their own or their opponent's pieces. **Pawns have a fighting value of 1 point.**

If a Pawn gets across the board to the opponent's back rank, it can be promoted to any piece, except a King.

Knight

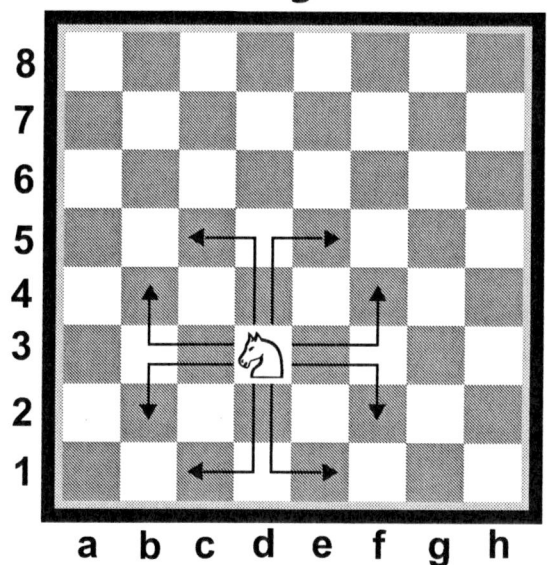

Knights move in an L-shape, 2 steps forward and one to the side. Knights move in all directions. They are the only piece that can jump over other pieces. The Knights are the only pieces on the back rank that can move out before a Pawn moves. Knights are powerful at the beginning of a game, when the board is crowded. **Knights have a fighting value of 3 points.**

Remember, a Knight always moves to the opposite color square. If it starts on a light square, it will land on a dark square. If it starts on a dark square, it will land on a light square. This is important when planning your Knight's moves.

A Knight in the center of the board attacks or defends 8 different squares. If you move to the sides and corners of the board, Knights are less powerful, attacking or defending only 2, 3 or 4 squares. A Knight's most powerful maneuver is the *fork,* an attack on more than one piece at a time.

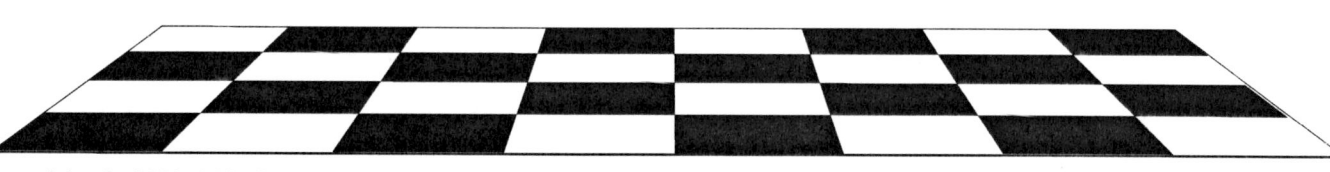

Bishop

Bishops move only on the diagonal, but can move forward or backward as many squares as possible, unless blocked by their own piece.

Each player has 2 Bishops — one starts on a light square, the other on a dark square. Moving only on a diagonal, the Bishop on a light square can never attack or defend a dark square; and, a Bishop on a dark square can never move to a light square.

Bishops attack or defend more squares when at the center of the board than at the side. It's important to develop your Bishops early in the game. **Bishops have a fighting value of 3 points.**

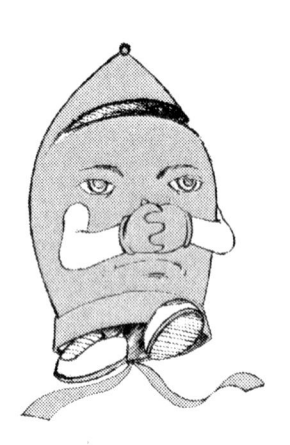

Rook

Rooks move horizontally, in either direction, and vertically up and down files. They move as far as they want unless their path is blocked. Rooks are equally powerful in the center or on the sides of the board. **Rooks have a fighting value of 5 points.**

Rooks should be one of the last pieces to be developed. They are especially powerful at the end of the game and play special roles in protecting your King and in checkmating your opponent's King.

Copyright © 2002, 2005 Teachable Tech, Inc.
All Rights Reserved.

The Basics:
Moves and Captures

Queen

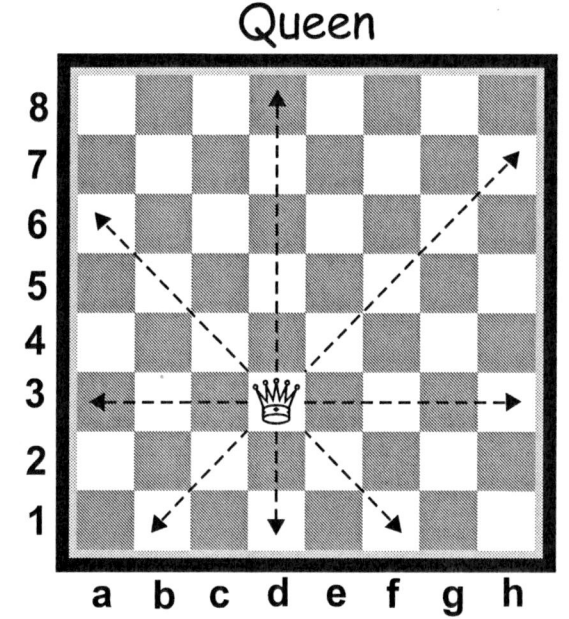

The Queen is the most powerful piece on the chessboard. She moves backwards or forwards on the vertical, horizontal or diagonal, as long as her path is not blocked. **The Queen has a fighting value of 9 points.**

The Queen is the only piece that can force the opponent's King to the edge of the board without assistance.

When a Pawn reaches your opponent's back rank, you most often promote it to a Queen — "queening a Pawn." You can have as many as 9 Queens on the board. But, remember, Queens are so powerful that they stop many King moves and can easily get you into stalemate rather than checkmate.

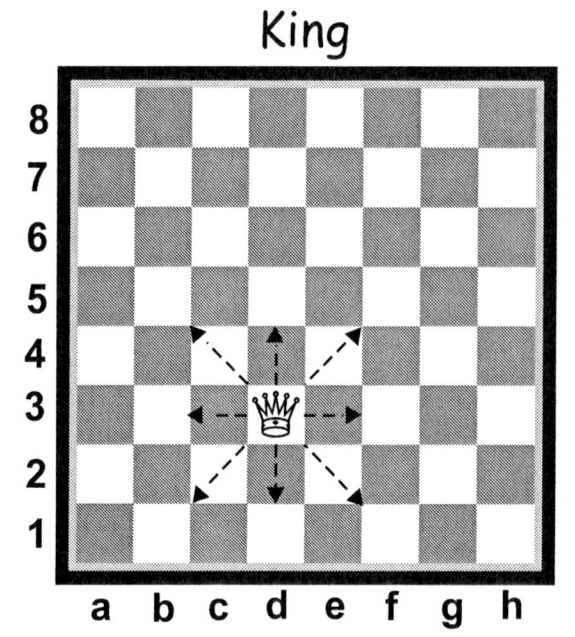

King

The King is the most important piece on the chessboard. It can move in any direction on the board, but can move only 1 square at a time.

If your King is under attack and you cannot escape, capture the attacking piece, or block the attack, it's checkmate and the game is over.

The King can never be captured or removed from the board and can never be moved into danger. If, at the end of the game, there are only 2 Kings left on the board, it's an automatic draw.

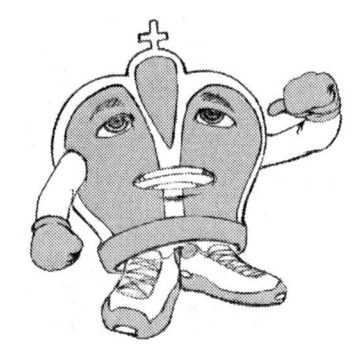

Special Pawn Move: En Passant

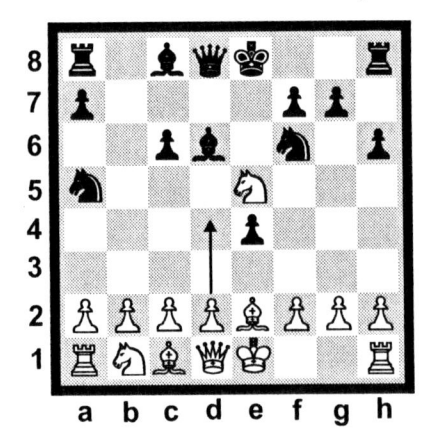

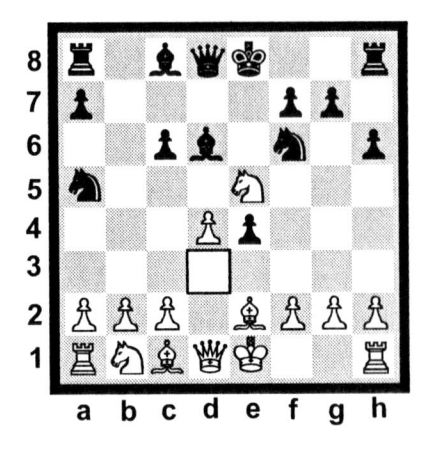

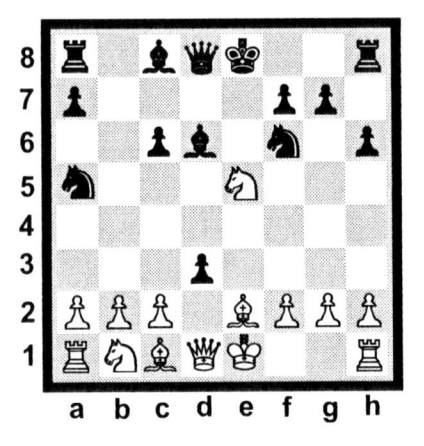

On its first move, a Pawn may move 1 or 2 squares. If a Pawn moves 2 squares and passes through a square that is "attacked" by an opponent's Pawn, it may be captured *en passant*.

The capture takes place as if the Pawn had moved only 1 square. The opponent's Pawn moves to the "attacked" square and removes the captured Pawn from the board. Capturing *en passant* can happen only on the opponent's next move. An opponent does not have to capture *en passant*.

Note: See page 23 for further explanation.

Special Pawn Move: Castling

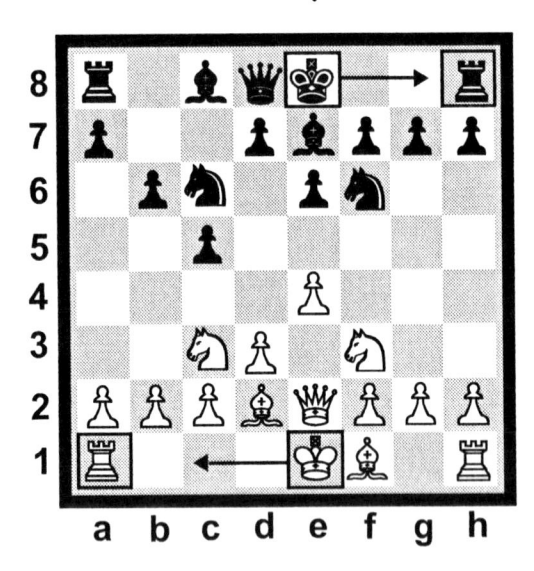

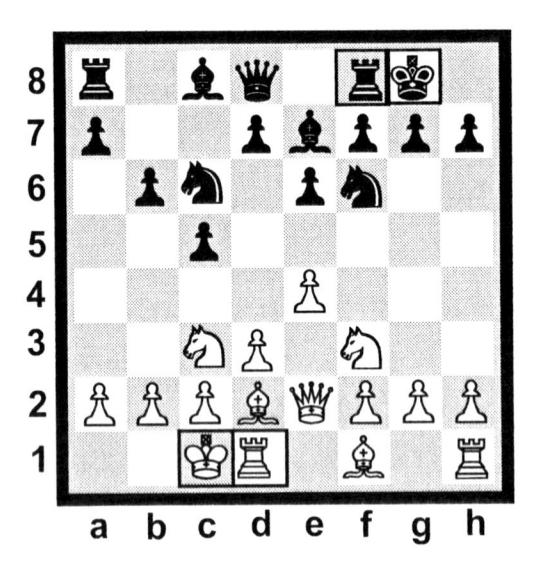

Castling is a good way to keep the King safe and to develop Rooks. It happens only if neither the King nor the Rook has been moved and the squares between them are empty. You cannot castle out of check, into check or through check.

Castling Kingside: The King moves 2 spaces toward the Rook. The Rook moves to the other side of the King.

Castling Queenside: The King moves 2 spaces toward the Rook. The Rook moves to the other side of the King.

The Basics: Rules of Chess

It's chess etiquette to shake hands before and after a game and to announce check or mate.

Set Up

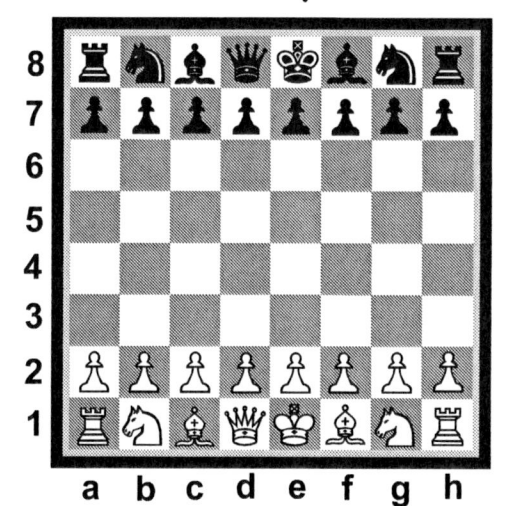

Chess is a game for 2 players. One has the White pieces at ranks 1 and 2; one has the Black pieces at ranks 7 and 8. Kings and Queens stand directly opposite each other. Queen's stand on their "color." Black Queen on dark square; White Queen on light square.

Note: If your board does not have numbered and lettered ranks and files, be sure that a light square is on the corner at your right hand side ("light on right").

Object of the Game

The main goal of the game is to checkmate your opponent's King. If your King is in check (attacked, but able to escape), it is illegal to make a move that does not get him out of check. No King is ever captured and removed from the board.

If it's your turn and your King nor any of your pieces can legally move, it is stalemate.

Basic Rules of Play

1. White always moves first, then players take turns moving.
2. You can move only one piece on a turn, except when castling. (See page 142.)
3. You capture an opponent's piece by moving to the square it occupies and removing it from the board. You can never move to a square occupied by your own piece. You may choose not to capture your opponent's piece and make a different move.
4. You may never pass. If you have a legal move, even if it is a "bad" move, you must make it. If you have no legal moves, the game ends in a draw.
5. **Touch/Move:** If you touch a piece, that's the piece you must move, as long as it is a legal move. If you remove your hand from a piece, that is where it must stay, if it is a legal move. If you do not remove your hand from the piece, you may move the piece you have touched to a different square, if it is a legal move. Your turn ends as soon as you remove your hand from the moved piece.
6. **Touch/Capture:** If you touch an opponent's piece that you can legally capture, you must capture it.

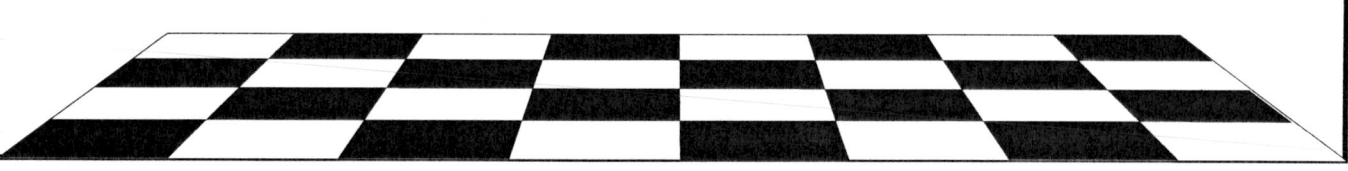

The Basics: Moves and Captures

7. If the game proceeds to the point where each side has only a King, this is a draw. If each side has only a King and a Bishop or only a King and 1 or 2 Knights, neither player has sufficient mating material and it's a draw. Sufficient material includes a King and a Pawn (the Pawn could become a Queen), a King and a Queen, and a King and a Rook.

8. If your opponent brings a clock or, if the tournament director (T.D.) places one on your table, you must use the clock.

    ♚ In rated chess games, each player will have at least 30 minutes for the game.

    ♚ Chess is played with one hand. Whichever hand you use to move the pieces is the same hand you will use to stop your clock.

    ♚ In a timed game, when your opponent's time has expired, it is your responsibility to stop both clocks. You claim a win, if you have sufficient mating material. If not, you claim a draw.

9. The 50-move rule is in effect only if a player records the game. Then, if in the last 50 moves for both sides, there has been neither a Pawn move nor the capture of any piece, a draw may be claimed. This is very rare.

10. When the exact position on the board is repeated 3 times with the same player to move, that player may call a draw.

Note: Tournaments and clubs will have their own rules of play, including time limits, notation and calls for arbitration. Be sure you are aware of these rules.

Glossary

algebraic grid: chess notation which uses lower case letters and numbers to describe squares on a chessboard; read in the same way as a graph with an x-y axis.

attack: a threat to capture an opponent's piece

battery: the doubling of forces such as, when a Queen and Bishop, Rook and Rook, or Queen and Rook are lined up together to strengthen power of an attack

blocked: pieces whose movement is limited because other pieces (usually of the same color) are in the way; anything can block a Pawn

bye: in tournament play, if there is an uneven number of players, the lowest rated player will get a full point without playing because it is not the player's fault that there is no one to challenge. Often, a half-point bye is given to a player who announces in advance that he or she must miss a round during the tournament.

candidate moves: moves that look like viable possibilities

capture: removal of your opponent's piece from the chessboard

castling: 2 moves in 1 turn, usually to place the King in a square safe from attack and to develop a Rook; castling takes place Kingside or Queenside

castling by hand: usually takes place if the King is forced to move before castling; takes several moves to get the King to safety without blocking the Rook

center: the 4 squares in the center of the board: d4, e4, d5 and e5; also called the red zone

check: the King is under attack

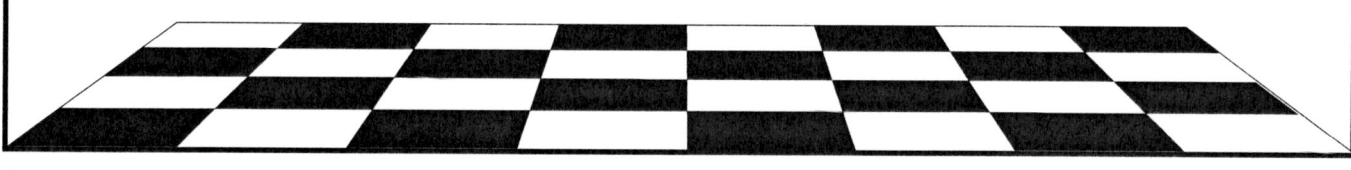

checkmate (mate): any position where the King is under attack and cannot avoid capture by blocking, fleeing or capturing

closed game: center Pawns are blocked and do not trade; a *closed game* prevents the easy movement of pieces across the board.

development: moving pieces from their original squares to positions where they can further the player's aims

discovered attack: occurs when one piece moves, exposing an attack by the piece it once blocked; the attacking piece does not move. In a *discovered check*, the piece which was once blocked is attacking the King

double attack: attacking 2 pieces at the same time with one move (See *fork*)

double-edged game: both sides have sharp attacking possibilities, usually an *open game*

draw: a tie game, where neither side wins or loses because they agree to a draw, they lack mating material, or there is a stalemate

en passant: (French for "in passing") special capture power by a Pawn of a Pawn when the latter advances 2 squares on its first move

escape: flee; move away from an opponent's attack and out of danger

file: vertical row of squares, named by lower case letters a – h

fork: attack on 2 pieces at the same time by 1 piece or Pawn

main line: the principal set of moves used in an opening (See *variation.*)

middle game: moves made and pieces developed after the opening and before the endgame; usually tactical moves

major pieces: the Rooks and the Queen

minor pieces: the Bishops and the Knights

move: shift of a chess piece from one square to another

near-center: the 12 squares surrounding the center: c3, d3, e3, f3, f4, f5, f6, e6, d6, c6, c5 and c4; See "center"

notation: method of recording chess games

open game: center Pawns trade early; files are opened to allow more rapid movement of pieces across the board

opening: first part of the game when players have a plan to develop their pieces to advantage; most openings have names

outpost: a protected piece, often a Knight, that is on a square that Pawns cannot attack easily; usually located near the opponent's King

passed Pawn: there is no opposing Pawn on the same file or on the files to the left or right that could block or capture

Pawn promotion: a pawn that successfully reaches an opponent's back rank is exchanged for a Queen, Rook, Knight or Bishop at that square

piling on: applying more pressure to a pinned piece by attacking again

pin: an attack against 2 or more of an opponent's pieces in a straight line — diagonal, rank or file — where the piece behind is of greater value, so if the front piece (the *pinned piece*) moves, there is greater loss. (An *absolute pin* occurs when the pinned piece is blocking the King and cannot legally move.)

positional player: one who prefers closed games to give them time to exploit small advantages to consolidate a winning position.

"power of 10": White's opening move (e2 to e4) gives the Queen 4 possible moves, the Bishop 5 and the Knight 1 additional move — 10 new moves.

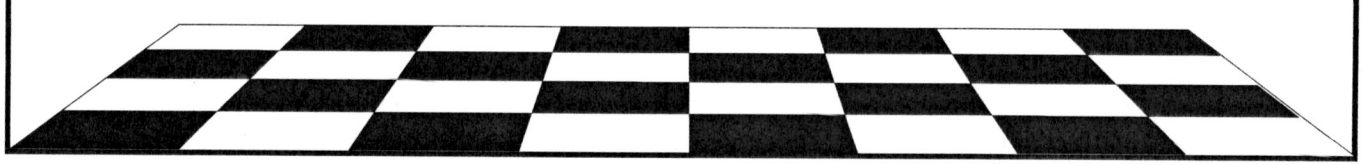

rank: horizontal row of squares on a chessboard, named by numbers 1 – 8

the red zone: another name for the 4 center squares; see "center"

remove the guard: tactic often used to gain an advantage and take a protecting piece from the opponent

stalemate: a game that ends when the player whose turn it is has no possible legal moves with any piece and the King is not in check

strategy: any long-range outline of a plan for future moves to win

tactical player: one who prefers open games and uses traps, threats and plans based on combinations or variations to establish a winning position; often, a gambit player.

tactics: combination of short-term moves, leading to a better position or material gain

takeback move: illegal; is used only in computer games

touch/move rule: once a player touches a piece, he or she must move it if there is a legal move

touch/capture rule: once a player touches an opponent's piece, he or she must capture it if there is a legal capture

trap: a move with a hidden danger for the opponent

variation: a set of moves that vary from the main line of an opening

Resources

Buying Tip: Most chess books are in paperback editions and often can be found in used bookstores and online.

Books
For Beginners

Alexander, C.H. O'D., and T.J. Beach. *Learn Chess: A New Way for All, Vol. I: First Principles.* 1987.

Fischer, Bobby. *Bobby Fischer Teaches Chess.* 1992.

Schneider, Stephen A. *Chess Basics, Scholastic Chess Series*, 2nd ed. 2005. (optional video/DVD)

Waitzkin, Fred. *Searching for Bobby Fischer: The Father of a Prodigy Observes the World of Chess.* 1993. (also, check out the Paramount film of the same name that is based on this book.)

Wilson, Fred. *101 Questions on How to Play Chess.* 1995.

Openings

De Frimian, Nick, et al, ed. *Modern Chess Openings.* 1999.

Horowitz, I.A., and Fred Reinfield. *How to Think Ahead in Chess.* 1977.
Nunn, John. *Nunn's Chess Openings.* 1999.

Pandolfini, Bruce. *Chess Openings: Traps and Zaps.* 1989.

Schneider, Stephen A. *Chess Openings I, Scholastic Chess Series*, 2nd ed. 2005. (optional video/DVD)

Middle Game — Tactics

Bain, John A. *Chess Tactics.* 1994.

Chandler, Murray. *How to Beat Your Dad at Chess.* 1998.

Pandolfini, Bruce. *Beginning Chess.* 1993.

Pandolfini, Bruce. *Chess Target Practice.* 1994.

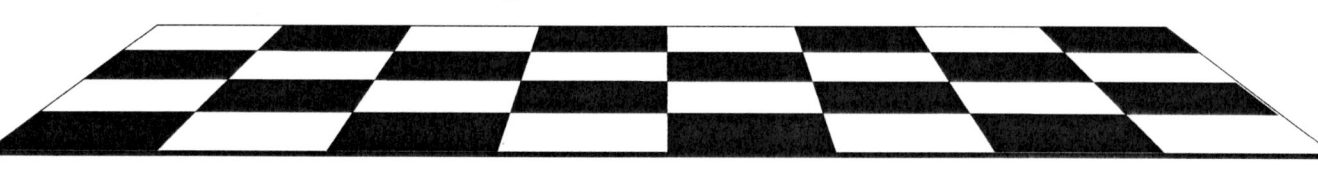

Resources

Reinfield, Fred. *1001 Brilliant Ways to Checkmate.* 1983.

Reinfield, Fred. *1001 Winning Chess Sacrifices and Combinations.* 1969.

Schneider, Stephen A. *Chess Puzzles: Tactics for the Beginner, Scholastic Chess Series.* 2005.

Endgame

Horowitz, I.A. *How to Win in the Chess Endings.* 1977.

Pandolfini, Bruce. *Pandolfini's Endgame Course.* 1988.

Schneider, Stephen A. *Endgames Strategies I, Scholastic Chess Series*, 2nd ed. 2005. (optional video/DVD)

Advanced

Nimzowitsch, Aron, and Lou Hays. *My System: 21st Century Edition.* 1991.

Tal, Mikhail and Iakov Damsky, *Attack with Mikhail Tal*, 1995.

The Rules

Just, Tim, et al, eds. *U.S. Chess Federation Official Rules of Chess, Fifth Edition*, 2003.

Free Lessons on the Internet

Chess is Fun (http://www.princeton.edu/~jedwards/cif/chess.html)

ChessWise (http://www.chesswise.com/)

Chess Organizations

Join these national and/or state organizations and subscribe to their official magazines.

The U.S. Chess Federation (http://www.uschess.org)

State Organizations (http://www.uschess.org/directories/AffiliateSearch/)

CERTIFICATE OF ACHIEVEMENT

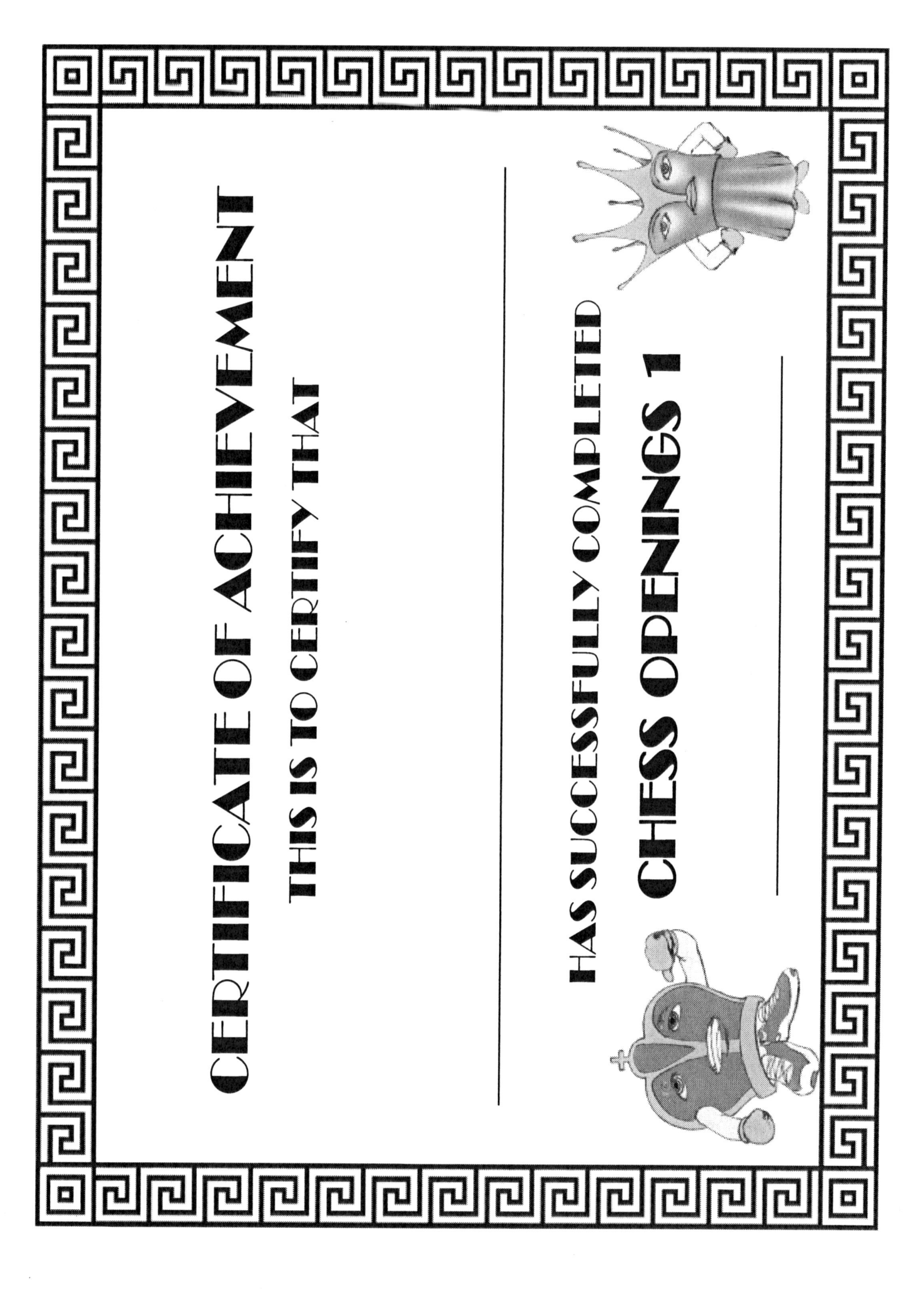

THIS IS TO CERTIFY THAT

HAS SUCCESSFULLY COMPLETED

CHESS OPENINGS 1

Workbook Guide for Chess Openings 1
Book 2: Scholastic Chess Series

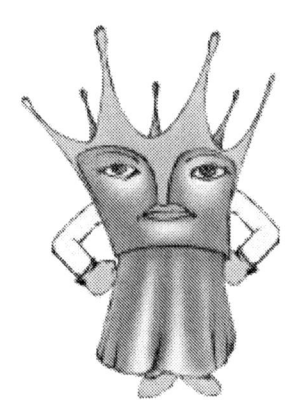

Every game starts with the opening. In *Chess Openings 1*, you'll find the things you need to know to take the advantage as the game begins — from basic strategies to detailed moves. A good opening sets the stage for a strong middle and endgame.

Tools for Chess Openings 1

The **workbook** is divided into chapters. Each chapter includes information to read and follow on a chessboard with activities and puzzles to do. And, the answers are provided on the following page.

Information is designed with easy-to-read graphic descriptions that clearly illustrate:
- step-by-step diagrams and notation for the opening moves
- key variations for scholastic players
- simple analysis of the moves and variations
- basic tactics — *pinning, forking* and *doubling up on the attack*

Activities and puzzles use easy-to-follow diagrams to practice new concepts. Answers and explanatory notes are found on the back of each page for immediate feedback.

The companion **video** or **DVD** features Steve Schneider, a successful scholastic chess coach for over 25 years. Coach Schneider walks you through each of the openings and their variations. As your own personal coach, he will guide you over the more complicated points and analyze the exciting moves, traps and tactics found in the openings.

Take advantage of the video coaching — stop the action when you need to work out moves, rewind and watch again. Come back after you've tried the opening in a game and look for the finer points. Coach Schneider follows the sequence of the chapters in your workbook, highlighting each section to introduce and enhance the readings and activities/puzzles, just as he does in his own classes.

- Video segments are short to provide plenty of time to work in the workbook and to play games. Chapter numbers, fonted in the right-hand corner of the screen, help you fast forward or rewind to the chapters you need or to review more difficult concepts.

- Video segments use the "Demo Board" to demonstrate concepts, provide examples and to clarify strategies.

- Video segments end with "It's Your Turn" to direct you to appropriate chapters for practice and reinforcement of specific concepts and skills.

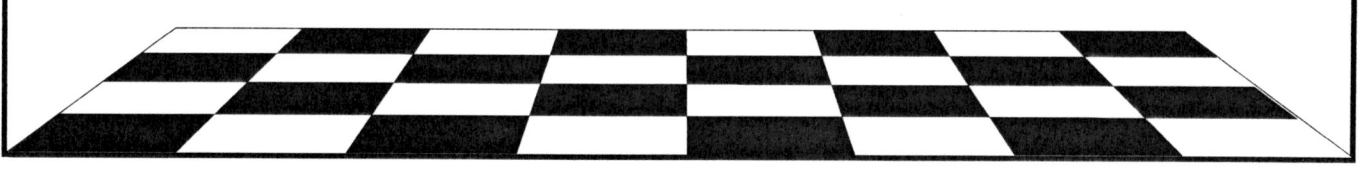

Note: The video segments and chapters follow a logical sequence for chess. However, for beginning scholastic players, we recommend using the Fork Trick, Chapter 7 and the Fried Liver, Chapter 8, as the final lessons. These chapters introduce the most complex variations in *Chess Openings 1*. For new players it's more important to have the breadth of the openings, including The Stonewall, rather than the depth that the Fork Trick and Fried Liver provide.

How to Use Chess Openings 1 at Home

Chess is a game for two, so it is most important that family or friends stay involved as you work through the book and video. If anyone needs a review of how the pieces move, capture and the rules of chess, check our new addition to the book: *The Basics*, page 139.

Older beginners can follow the video and workbook on their own.
- Watch the video segments before you begin each chapter.
- Follow the chapter diagrams using a chessboard and pieces, working through the moves for each opening or concept. We recommend that you use a tournament chessboard with numbers and letters to name ranks and files. Or, you can write file letters and rank numbers with a marker on your current chessboard.
- Try the activities and puzzles. Check your answers to see if you understand. If you have problems, watch the video and/or look over the readings once again.
- Play the openings again and again, as Black and as White. The only way to really understand an opening is to repeat it often. As you understand the reason for each move, you will see the logic of the moves and they will be easier to remember.
- See how quickly you can make the moves of an opening you have studied. Use a clock or timer.
- Find ways to continue or modify your opening plan based on your opponent's moves.

Younger beginners will need an older sibling or parent to guide them through the video and workbook.
- Watch a video segment together, then set up a chessboard to go over the information. Read through appropriate information in the workbook and take "Your Turn" to complete activities and puzzles.
- Even non-readers can work through the openings, but will need guidance throughout the workbook.
- Play the openings together, alternating color.
- Challenge the player to demonstrate an opening, moving the pieces for both colors as quickly as possible. Remember, "touch move": If the player makes a mistake, start again.

How to Use Chess Openings 1 in a Chess Club

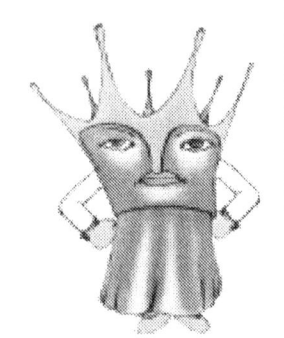

The Scholastic Chess Series is excellent for working with large groups, small groups or individuals. It is self-paced and can be self-directed. Groups have the greatest success when video instruction, readings and activities/puzzles are interspersed with many practice games.

The workbook is copyrighted and cannot be reproduced. Each member of the club must have his or her own copy of the workbook for *Chess Openings* 1. These may be purchased by the club and then distributed or parents may purchase them individually at www.championshipchess.net.

The goal of a chess club is to have fun as you learn. It will take many meetings for some players to go through only the first basic openings, while others are ready to move on more quickly. Divide group instruction according to abilities. It is not important to go through all of the chapters of *Chess Openings 1* with all of the club members. It is important to make sure that everyone understands and can apply the concepts in the openings they learn.

Video and Chapter Readings

Use a video segment to introduce each chapter and, then, direct club members to their workbook readings to reinforce the concept. Work in teams to go through the readings, using a chessboard to follow the notation and reproduce the diagrams.

— OR —

Set up a Demo Board to help illustrate openings and tactics. Review applicable video for reinforcement or enhancement.

Activities and Puzzles

Work through the activities and puzzles using the Demo Board; or, have teams use chessboards to explore the puzzles. Remind club members that answers and tips are provided on the back of each puzzle, so that they may correct themselves as they learn more about the concept.

— OR —

Use activities and puzzles as assessable review sheets for players to use to gain points and ranking in the club.

Chessboard, Pieces, Scorebooks and Clocks

Use **chessboards and pieces** throughout the workbook to test different variations and "play the game out" as directed.

Coaching Tip: To help with visualization, challenge students to describe the opening without the pieces, or even without a board. They should be able to say whether squares are dark or light.

Allow plenty of time for club members to explore the openings in their own games, playing both Black and White. You can only understand an opening thoroughly by playing it over many times.

Coaching Tip: Divide the group to play team consultation games.

Scorebooks provide opportunities to analyze games and decide which moves take the advantage and which ones lead to lost material or lost games. Recording their games allows review and analysis of their openings and responses.

Coaching Tip: You may want to invite another coach or strong player to help analyze the students' games.

It is important that beginners not try to use the **clocks** to play speed chess but to use them to practice **how** to use the clocks and to learn to budget their time. Throughout the book, we suggest playing from a specific position with players having 15 minutes each to play out the games. When playing a full game, each player should have at least 30 minutes. There are many positions throughout the book where it is important to play a few moves to test different possibilities. From these positions, 10 moves within 5 minutes for each player is sufficient time for study.

Testing

Test mastery of an opening by having club members demonstrate the moves for both Black and White from memory on a chessboard or Demo Board. Remember, it's "touch move," so if they make a mistake they start again.

Coaching Tip: Many players like to demonstrate how quickly they can make the memorized, main line moves. Set a timer and they'll compete with themselves to improve.

TIPS FOR USING THE DEMO BOARD (OPTIONAL)

Replicate openings, activities and puzzles from the workbook and video on the Demo Board. Use the board and erasable markers or stickers to illustrate ways to solve the problems or answer questions *before players try them on their own,* or as a means of sharing answers after they have completed them individually.

Use the Demo Board for instructional time. Then, use workbook activities and/or chessboards and pieces to practice using the new information.

Challenge players to use the Demo Board to illustrate their games and have the group analyze the moves.

TIPS FOR PLAYING GAMES IN THE CLUB

Have players decide who's White and who's Black by having one player hold a White Pawn and a Black Pawn behind his or her back. The other player chooses a hand and plays the corresponding color. In subsequent games, have players switch colors with their opponents.

Keep a class chart to track play. Since these are practice games, it is less important to track who wins and more important to track who's playing whom.

Track play for 3 to 5 games. Those who win the most games will be in the top group and will continue to play each other. Others will form a second group. This makes tracking play more manageable. The top group may start off smaller so that others can move up into it.

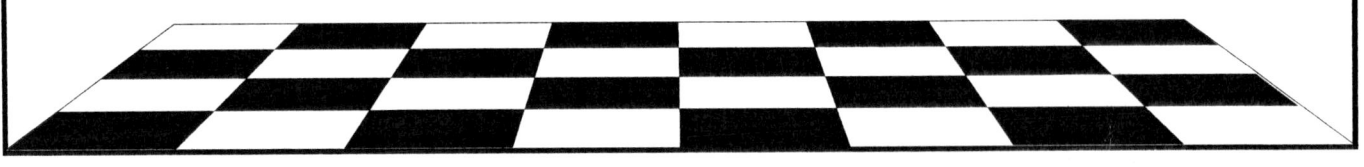

How to Organize a Successful School Chess Club

Getting Started

You'll need to obtain permission for the club from the Principal. These are some of the logistics you'll need to discuss:

- School chess clubs should meet at least once a week — before or after school or even at lunchtime. Set the time and day and plan ways to notify students and their parents.
- The chess club should be an opportunity for play and instruction and a chance to find out updates about appropriate tournaments, camps and other clubs.
- The club may be open to all students or only open to a segment of the school population.
- The chess club could collect dues or participate in fundraisers to pay for materials — chess sets, beginning chess books (no clocks needed in the beginning) some small awards and an end-of-the-year party.
- Plan to send a note home to parents asking for parent volunteers. Volunteers can assist in management — track games, record attendance, manage the chess ladder, etc.

Running the Club

Chess clubs can be informal settings where students come and play. Or, a club can be a more formal setting with an emphasis on more competitive play, instruction and improving skills. Both types of groups should follow the rules of chess, including "touch move."

- As part of the first chess meetings, have a tournament to rank the players. Each student should play 3 games to set the rankings. This tournament could continue over 3 meetings.
    - It doesn't matter who plays whom in the first round.
    - In the second and third rounds, those who have won should play others who have won; those who have lost, play others who have lost; those who have tied play others who have tied, as long as they don't play the same person again.
- In tournament play, students get 1 point for a win, a half-point for a draw. If a player is absent, he or she can be given a half-point draw. If there's an uneven number, one of the players with the lowest score gets a full-point "bye" because it's not their fault that there's no one for them to challenge.

    This sets up the rankings. With a large group you might have more than one tournament — perhaps by grade level (never by gender). There should be at least 12 in a group.

- From the tournament you can set up a chess ladder. The simplest way is to write the rankings on paper or poster board. You could get more sophisticated by using Popsicle sticks or using refrigerator magnets with students' pictures and a metal board.
    - Students can challenge 5 or fewer up the ladder.
    - A person has to accept only one challenge per week.
    - The person being challenged gets to choose color.
    - If the challenger wins, the players swap places on the ladder.

    (Frequent absences can make it more difficult for students to move up the ladder. Students who do not attend club regularly should be placed at the bottom of the ladder.)

Note: Set up a "bomb ladder" so that any loss places a player at the bottom. Or, set up a modified bomb where, if the #1 ranked player loses, only he/she goes to the bottom of the ladder.

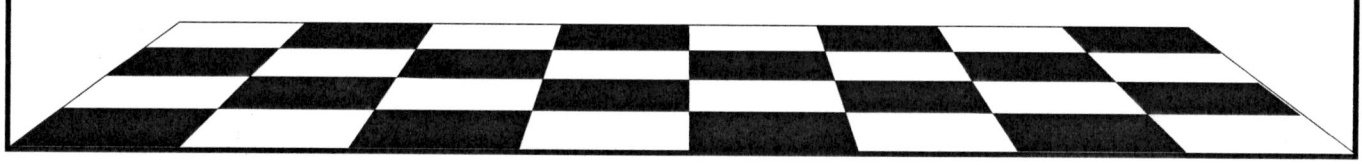

Students need to report their results to the sponsor and should not be allowed to change the ladder themselves.
- The chess ladder is only one way to recognize students. Participation and achievement may also be rewarded through a point system:
    o Students who demonstrate success at specific skills or openings
    o Students who participate in outside tournaments or community clubs

Your point system may promote students from Pawn to Knight to Rook, etc.

Promoting the Club

Once the structure of the club is set, there are many possible ways to promote a successful club.
- For the first month, only players who know how to play may take part. Then, have an open house to invite others in to learn to play. Students could act as peer coaches.
- If you want to make chess a popular sport in the school, you may want to put chess sets in classrooms or in the media center.
- Students can create posters about chess to distribute around the school. They can go to different classes and "market" chess — tutoring or introducing interesting facts about this ancient game.
- Plan a "Chess is Fun" afternoon or evening and invite other schools to come and compete. No scores need to be kept, but everyone has fun.

Rooks Rule!

Video Selection Chart

Video Segment	Time	Start	End	Student Pages: Pages	Student Pages: Activity #'s
Chapter 1: Opening Theory	1:55	:20	2:15	1 - 8	1 & 2
Chapter 2: Chess Notation: An Introduction	4:25	2:20	6:45	9 - 20	3 & 4
Chapter 3: Chess Notation: Capturing & Special Moves	4:55	6:50	11:45	21 - 32	5 - 7
Chapter 4: The Queen's Raid	5:55	11:50	18:05	33 - 58	8 - 15
Chapter 5: En Passant	2:30	18:10	20:40	59 - 60	16
Chapter 6A: Two Knights Defense (Part 1)	5:45	20:45	26:00	61 - 68	17 - 18
Chapter 6B: Two Knights Defense (Part 2)	6:00	26:05	32:05	69 - 82	19 - 23
Chapter 7: The Fork Trick	3:50	32:10	36:00	83 - 94	24 - 25
Chapter 8: Fried Liver Attack	4:00	36:05	40:05	95 - 106	26 - 29
Chapter 9: Power of the Pin	3:50	40:10	44:00	107 - 112	30 - 31
Chapter 10: The Stonewall	11:55	44:05	56:00	113 - 132	32 - 37
Chapter 11: Taking Advantage in the Opening	3:55	56:05	1:00:00	133 - 138	38 - 39